Why is America Going Back to the Moon?

By Mark R. Whittington

For Jayney, who taught me that while sometimes you won't get what you want, you may finally get what you need.

Introduction

Why go back to the moon? Haven't we been there, done that? It's a question most often asked by people who don't think space exploration by humans is a sensible idea, or they think that because Americans have been to the moon, over 50 years ago, it is time to send astronauts to someplace more interesting, such as Mars.

The answer to that question depends on how one views the exploration and economic exploitation of space. If one thinks that a space program is something good to have, something a great power does because it is a great power, the answer would be one thing. If one thinks that the primary goal of space exploration is the garnering of scientific knowledge, the answer may be something else. If the goal of a space program is primarily national prestige, then the answer might be another thing.

One of the more current reasons for going back to the moon is the opportunity it represents for commerce. That opportunity ranges from tourism to mining the moon's abundant natural resources. The idea that money can be made on the high frontier has increased interest in exploring it.

Public spending on civil space has always been a bargain. Technological spinoffs have been a net income producer for the American economy. The argument has proven triggering for people of a libertarian bent. Why not just spend the money on a research and development tax cut and get the new technology directly? Good luck arguing that back in the 1960s. One of the great things about the Apollo program was that the money spent on it was not spent on the twin disasters of that decade, Vietnam, and the War on Poverty.

The greatest development of the 21st century has been the rise of space billionaires, such as SpaceX's Elon Musk and Blue Origin's and Amazon's Jeff Bezos, who have been willing to pour their own money into what amounts to private space programs. SpaceX and Blue Origin have made money being contractors for NASA and the military. But both companies have grand plans that involve space settlements, expanding humanity out beyond the confines of Earth.

Why would a couple of high-tech internet entrepreneurs try to make space travel a paying business? Partly because they think they can make money doing it. But partly, they and others are building rockets because, inspired as they were by Apollo and *Star Trek*, they think that space is so utterly cool that no more enjoyable way exists to make money and have fun doing it.

Sooner than anyone imagines, decisions about whether and how we explore space will no longer be the sole province of elected politicians and government bureaucrats. Human civilization had best adjust itself to the new reality. Governments can help by providing core markets or, at least, get out of the way.

Of course, even with the rise of companies such as SpaceX and Blue Origin, NASA will still have a major role in space exploration. Indeed, NASA has forged bonds of mutual benefit with commercial space companies. The space agency regards the space billionaires as partners and not as competitors. Hence, Artemis, the program to return Americans to the moon and then on to Mars, bears only a passing resemblance to Apollo.

Also, unlike Apollo, Artemis is an international program. The United States first invited international partners such as Canada, the European Union, and Japan to participate in the project that eventually became the International Space Station. Later, NASA took on Russia as a space station partner. The United States pursues a similar strategy with the Artemis program. Space as an instrument of international diplomacy creates an entirely new dimension to the question of why we should return to the moon.

Why should we return to the moon is a question that must be answered so convincingly that it will stand up through changes in Congresses and presidencies. While President Trump initiated the Artemis program, he has been replaced by Joe Biden, an elderly president whose initial executive orders seem designed to erase the legacy of his predecessor. Will Artemis be among the achievements of Donald Trump that will be consigned to the ash heap of history? Or will the arguments for continuing to return to the moon be so profound and irrefutable that even Biden will be compelled to continue the effort? History awaits the answer to that question.

Going to the Moon and Back Again

Chapter 1 – Why America Went to the Moon the First Time

1961-1972

By May 25, 1961, the new John F. Kennedy presidency was in considerable trouble. A series of missteps and one singular event had cast doubt on the young president's ability to shape events to the advantage of the United States.

The Kennedy Administration was still reeling from the effects of the Bay of Pigs invasion, a mission beset by failures in planning and operation. The plan was to land a force of militarily trained Cuban exiles at the Bay of Pigs, Cuba. The sudden appearance of an armed force, it was thought, would cause an uprising against the communist regime of Fidel Castro and lead to the liberation of the island nation.

Instead, the hoped-for uprising failed to materialize, and the Cuban Army defeated the invasion in detail. The fact that President Kennedy withheld planned-for air support at the last minute in a vain attempt to obscure American fingerprints on the invasion did not help.

To make matter worse, on April 12, 1961, the Soviets launched Cosmonaut Yuri Gagarin into low Earth orbit, scoring yet another space first against the United States in a series that started with the first satellite launch in 1957. The fact that American astronaut Alan Shepard flew in a suborbital flight on May 5, did little to lessen the sting of the Soviet feat.

Clearly, something had to be done to change the narrative of the United States being beaten and humiliated at every turn. The Kennedy Administration had just the plan, which the president intended to roll out during a speech before a joint session of Congress on the evening of May 25.

The speech contained a laundry list of what President Kennedy considered national needs. However, all that anyone remembers is the following:

"First, I believe that this nation should commit itself to achieving the goal, before this decade is out, of landing a man on the moon and returning him safely to the earth. No single space project in this period will be more impressive to mankind, or more important for the long-range exploration of space; and none will be so difficult or expensive to accomplish."[i]

Why did President Kennedy throw down the gauntlet and declare a race to the moon? The key part of the paragraph was the phrase "more impressive to mankind." Kennedy was aware that the series of Soviet space firsts endangered the United States because they suggested that the future did not reside in America, with its traditions of freedom and tolerance, but rather in the Soviet Union. However, a mission to the moon would be so impressive, so awesome that no one on the planet, even those behind the Iron Curtain, could but believe that the United States owned the future.

Kennedy had already made the connection of achievements in space to the future on Earth several paragraphs before. "Now it is time to take longer strides--time for a great new American enterprise--time for this nation to take a clearly leading role in space achievement, which in many ways may hold the key to our future on Earth."

Over a year later, on October 12, 1962, President Kennedy addressed a crowd at Rice Stadium in Houston, Texas, and expanded his arguments for going to the moon. The speech was filled with a celebration of America's pioneering and scientific past. It was delivered long before academics and educators shifted to the Howard Zinn narrative of American history being filled with victims, particularly Native Americans and African American slaves, rather than heroic pioneers and settlers. [ii]

Kennedy cast the space race as a contest between tyranny and freedom.

"Those who came before us made certain that this country rode the first waves of the industrial revolutions, the first waves of modern invention, and the first wave of nuclear power, and this generation does not intend to founder in the backwash of the coming age of space. We mean to be a part of it--we mean to lead it. For the eyes of the world now look into space, to the moon and to the planets beyond, and we have vowed that we shall not see it governed by a hostile flag of conquest, but by a banner of freedom and peace. We have vowed that we shall not see space filled with weapons of mass destruction, but with instruments of knowledge and understanding."

Kennedy went on to point out:

"Yet the vows of this nation can only be fulfilled if we in this nation are first, and, therefore, we intend to be first. In short, our leadership in science and in industry, our hopes for peace and security, our obligations to ourselves as well as others, all require us to make this effort, to solve these mysteries, to solve them for the good of all men, and to become the world's leading space-faring nation."

Then the president presented his vision of a new age of space exploration.

"We set sail on this new sea because there is new knowledge to be gained, and new rights to be won, and they must be won and used for the progress of all people. For space science, like nuclear science and all technology, has no conscience of its own. Whether it will become a force for good or ill depends on man, and only if the United States occupies a position of pre-eminence can we help decide whether this new ocean will be a sea of peace or a new, terrifying theater of war. I do not say that we should or will go unprotected against the hostile misuse of space any more than we go unprotected against the hostile use of land or sea, but I do say that space can be explored and mastered without feeding the fires of war, without repeating the mistakes that man has made in extending his writ around this globe of ours."

The implication could not be clearer. If the Soviet Union were to win the space race, that country would use its victory as a means to dominate the planet and advance its goal to spread communism across the planet. If the United States won, then space would be a venue of peaceful exploration and scientific discovery that would benefit everyone.

Kennedy also suggested that going to the moon was a worthy thing for its own sake, something that strengthens and improves the country that undertakes it.

"There is no strife, no prejudice, no national conflict in outer space as yet. Its hazards are hostile to us all. Its conquest deserves the best of all mankind, and its opportunity for peaceful cooperation may never come again. But why, some say, the moon? Why choose this as our goal? And they may well ask, why climb the highest mountain? Why, 35 years ago, fly the Atlantic? Why does Rice play Texas?

"We choose to go to the moon. We choose to go to the moon in this decade and do the other things, not because they are easy, but because they are hard, because that goal will serve to organize and measure the best of our energies and skills, because that challenge is one that we are willing to accept, one we are unwilling to postpone, and one which we intend to win, and the others, too."

Kennedy went on to mention some of the educational, technological, and economic benefits of going to the moon, arguments that would be echoed by space proponents for decades going forward.

"The growth of our science and education will be enriched by new knowledge of our universe and environment, by new techniques of learning and mapping and observation, by new tools and computers for industry, medicine, the home as well as the school. Technical institutions, such as Rice, will reap the harvest of these gains.

"And finally, the space effort itself, while still in its infancy, has already created a great number of new companies, and tens of thousands of new jobs. Space and related industries are generating new demands in investment and skilled personnel, and this city and this State, and this region, will share greatly in this growth. What was once the furthest outpost on the old frontier of the West will be the furthest outpost on the new frontier of science and space. Houston, your City of Houston, with its Manned Spacecraft Center, will become the heart of a large scientific and engineering community. During the next 5 years the National Aeronautics and Space Administration expects to double the number of scientists and engineers in this area, to increase its outlays for salaries and expenses to $60 million a year; to invest some $200 million in plant and laboratory facilities; and to direct or contract for new space efforts over $1 billion from this Center in this City."

In the very next paragraph, Kennedy admitted, "I realize that this is in some measure an act of faith and vision, for we do not now know what benefits await us."

Less than a year later, in a September 18, 1963 meeting with NASA Administrator Jim Webb. Kennedy had begun to express doubts about the Apollo program. Both political and media opposition to the project had started to increase due to mounting costs. Kennedy was concerned what effect the developing pushback down have on his prospects of being reelected in 1964.

Space historian John Logsdon wrote an extensive analysis of the meeting, revealed in an audio tape released by the JFK library.[iii] Kennedy and Webb mulled tying the Apollo program to national security, in effect making it a military program. Kennedy also mused about how the race to the moon might present "-- the kind of improvements in our national life which will come from this—the leadership of the United States and the national security we'll get from it—all those factors."

In a September 20, 1963 address to the UN General Assembly, President Kennedy tried another approach and offered something of an olive branch to the Soviets.[iv]

"Finally, in a field where the United States and the Soviet Union have a special capacity--in the field of space--there is room for new cooperation, for further joint efforts in the regulation and exploration of space. I include among these possibilities a joint expedition to the moon. Space offers no problems of sovereignty; by resolution of this Assembly, the members of the United Nations have foresworn any claim to territorial rights in outer space or on celestial bodies and declared that international law and the United Nations Charter will apply. Why, therefore, should man's first flight to the moon be a matter of national competition? Why should the United States and the Soviet Union, in preparing for such expeditions, become involved in immense duplications of research, construction, and expenditure? Surely we should explore whether the scientists and astronauts of our two countries--indeed of all the world--cannot work together in the conquest of space, sending someday in this decade to the moon not the representatives of a single nation, but the representatives of all of our countries."

Kennedy had a couple of reasons for this gambit.

The Cuban Missile Crisis, which very nearly resulted in a nuclear war between the United States and the Soviet Union, frightened Kennedy, and his advisors. The strategy of confrontation with the Soviets changed to one of de-escalation. The two superpowers had already formed a Nuclear Test Ban Treaty and established a direct hotline between the White House and the Kremlin. Why not change the space race into a space cooperation mission, one that would forge bonds between the two superpowers and thus further the cause of peace?

The other reason, related to the decline in political support, was that the Kennedy Administration was beginning to get sticker shock at the cost of racing the Soviets to the moon. Some members of Congress certainly were. Just before Kennedy was assassinated, a Senate committee at the behest of Senator William Proxmire, D-Wisconsin, voted to cut funding for the Apollo moon program, setting the lunar landing goal by the end of the 1960s very much in doubt.

Logsdon notes that Kennedy regained his enthusiasm for the Apollo program during a visit to Cape Canaveral on November 16, 1963. He was able to see solid, tangible progress in the race to the moon. Had Kennedy lived, it is very likely to would have fought for the Apollo program with renewed vigor, both in the halls of Congress and on the campaign trail.

Then President Kennedy met his end in Dallas on November 22, 1963. The Apollo moon landing program became a monument to the martyred president. The Senate restored the funding it had cut. The rest, as they say, is history.

I describe what happened afterwards in my previous book, "Why Is It So Hard to Go Back to the Moon?" It should be noted that Kennedy's original strategy of showing up the Soviet Union succeeded brilliantly. The Soviet leadership and people never recovered their self-confidence.

When President Ronald Reagan proposed a space-based missile defense system, known as the Strategic Defense Initiative and derided by Reagan's domestic political opponents as "Star

Wars," the Soviet leadership paid attention. The Americans had beaten the Soviets to the moon. They could make nuclear ICBMs obsolete as well.

The ensuing arms race broke the already rickety Soviet Union and led directly to the end of the Cold War. President John F. Kennedy's original strategy was more successful than even he likely imagined. The race to the moon lifted the spectre of global thermonuclear war and liberated tens of millions of people in Eastern Europe from Soviet tyranny.

As a bonus, according to an economic analysis by Chase Econometrics, every dollar spent on Apollo returned at least 14 dollars in increased GDP. All that money spent on space turned out to be a great investment, after all.

Chapter 2 - Why did President George H. W Bush want to return to the moon?

1989-1992

Twenty years to the day that human beings landed on the moon, the men who had accomplished that feat, Neil Armstrong, Buzz Aldrin, and Michael Collins, were gathered at a speaker's platform that had been set up just outside the Smithsonian Air and Space Museum in Washington, D.C. Another newly elected president, George H. W. Bush, was preparing to make a speech outlining America's next steps in space.

Many in the media and the political class opined at the time that the first President Bush was springing his proposal to return to the moon and send astronauts to Mars from out of the blue. But Bush's proposal was grounded on three years of studies, including the report of the National Commission on Space, entitled "Pioneering the Space Frontier,"[v] developed in the wake of the *Challenger* disaster in 1986.

Even nearly 35 years later, the report is a remarkable document. It laid out a systematic program for exploring and, more importantly, settling deep space, including the moon, Mars, and "accessible asteroids." The report included verbiage on international partnerships, developing commercial markets, and developing technology that could also have Earthly applications.

"Pioneering the Space Frontier" suggested a program whose goal was nothing less than establishing free societies on other worlds, where free enterprise would develop resources and create new industries. Considering that previous large-scale space programs such as Apollo, the space shuttle, and the then new space station project had narrower, more specific goals, the proposed deep space exploration program contained a vision that resonates today.

Succinctly, the benefits of expanding human civilization into the solar system were:

"The new space program we propose for 21st-century America will return tangible benefits in three forms:

• By "pulling-through" advances in science and technology of critical importance to the Nation's future economic strength and national security

• By providing direct economic returns from new space-based enterprises that capitalize upon broad, low-cost access to space, and

• By opening new worlds on the space frontier, with vast resources that can free humanity's aspirations from the limitations of our small planet of birth."

The following year, NASA issued a report called "Leadership and America's Future in Space"[vi] that was designed as a response to "Pioneering the Space Frontier." The Ride Report, as it was called after the chairperson of the NASA commission, Dr. Sally Ride, the first American woman in space, was somewhat light on rationales and heavy on mission proposals. However, the report did suggest that any space initiative have as its goal restoring American leadership in space, which in 1987 was seen as lacking,

The Ride Report attempted to define American leadership thus:

"Leadership cannot simply be proclaimed - it must be earned. As NASA evaluates its goals and objectives within the framework of the National Space Policy, the agency must first understand what is required to "maintain U.S. space leadership," since that understanding will direct the selection of national objectives.

"Leadership does not require that the U.S. be preeminent in all areas and disciplines of space enterprise. In fact, the broad spectrum of space activities and the increasing number of spacefaring nations make it virtually impossible for any nation to dominate in this way. Being an effective leader does mandate, however, that this country have capabilities which enable it to act independently and impressively when and where it chooses, and that its goals be capable of inspiring others - at home and abroad - to support them. It is essential for this country to move promptly to determine its priorities and to make conscious choices to pursue a set of objectives which will restore its leadership status.

"Leadership results from both the capabilities a country has acquired and the active demonstration of those capabilities; accordingly, the United States must have, and also be perceived as having, the ability to meet its goals and achieve its objectives."

What would be the benefits of such leadership?

"National pride and international prestige are two natural benefits of leadership in space. National pride grows as citizens recognize their country's abilities and achievements; international prestige rises as other nations recognize those abilities and achievements."

Against the backdrop of those reports, President George H. W. Bush ascended to the platform on that Washington summer day and delivered his speech committing America to go back to the moon and on to Mars.[vii]

President Bush's speech lingered for a considerable time on the glories of the past, understandable considering the presence of the Apollo 11 crew and the backdrop of a museum containing the artifacts of air and space technology, including the Columbia command module in which Armstrong, Aldrin, and Collins voyaged to the moon 20 years before. Bush's rationale for returning to the moon and going to Mars was more of an emotional appeal than a list of easily understood benefits.

"Why the Moon? Why Mars? Because it is humanity's destiny to strive, to seek, to find. And because it is America's destiny to lead."

In other words, Bush relied more on the Ride Report than Pioneering the Space Frontier to justify the heavy expense of a deep space exploration program.

Bush did not articulate another reason for starting a deep space exploration program. By 1989 his administration had already surmised that the Cold War was drawing to a close. Indeed, that autumn, the Berlin Wall would fall. By the end of the first Bush administration, the Soviet Union would be on the ash heap of history, fulfilling the dream of Bush's predecessor, President Ronald Reagan.

The end of the Cold War was a boon to all humankind, but it presented a practical, political problem. America's military industrial complex, the network of private companies that developed and built the weapons that would fight America's wars and deter the ultimate war that might destroy all of humankind would have far less to do than it did since the Cold War had started.

Clearly, something had to be done to prevent economic dislocation that would cost perhaps millions of registered voters their jobs and hundreds of campaign contributors their government contracts. Bush and his advisors concluded that a deep space exploration program would fit the bill nicely.

Of course, no politician would offer such a crass rationale out loud. But the reason existed and should have been enough to persuade politicians who had control of the federal government till.

The sad death of the Space Exploration Initiative, as Bush's proposal came to be called, is already set out in a document called The Mars Wars[viii] and my own "Why is it so Hard to Go Back to the Moon?"[ix]

Bush's speech and the aftermath do render some lessons when it comes to laying out reasons for going back to the moon or doing anything else that is difficult and costly. Feel good and nebulous rationales simply do not cut it. Bush and his speech writers should have gone back to the report of the National Commission on Space and used some of the reasons stated there to buttress the case for returning to the moon and going on to Mars. Economic growth and technology development are concepts people, even politicians, can understand. Concepts such as "leadership" and "national pride" turned out to be less persuasive.

The Space Exploration Initiative still may have failed because of other reasons, but at least a better case would have been made for it if the first Bush administration had communicated more concrete reasons for it.

It should be noted that President Bush attempted to revive support for the Space Exploration Initiative during a commencement address at Texas A & I University in Kingsville, Texas on May 11, 1990[x]. He attempted to trot out another rationale for exploring space, education.

"Our space program will, indeed, help rekindle public interest in science and mathematics, revitalize an area of our educational system that has become disturbingly weak. In fact, one of the education goals that Dr. Cavazos referred to, one that we announced in January, is to make the United States first in math and science by the year 2000."

Bush then added technology development as a rationale.

"But this space program will do more. It will revolutionize everything from computers to communications, from medicine to metals, regaining and retaining America's high-tech competitive edge. It will create new technologies, new industries, and new jobs."

Two phrases suggest themselves: Too little and too late. The reaction to the speech from both the media and the political class was all snark. Bush would have been better served to have used these and other reasons to explore space, including going back to the moon, in his original remarks. He ultimately could not persuade most Americans why they should go back to the moon.

Chapter 3 – Why did President George W. Bush want to go back to the moon?

2004-2009

People who gathered at NASA Headquarters in Washington on January 14, 2004 could be forgiven for feeling a sense of déjà vu. A president named George Bush was preparing to give a speech on space policy in the shadow of another shuttle disaster[xi]. Less than a year before, the space shuttle *Columbia* had broken apart in the skies over Texas, killing its crew, after a successful mission in low Earth orbit. The administration of George W. Bush had spent much of the ensuing time pondering what the *Columbia* disaster meant for space policy, having conversations with players at NASA and in Congress. The younger Bush had concluded that if brave astronauts must die in space, they should do so accomplishing grander things than going around in circles.

In short, just as Bush's father had concluded about 15 years before, it was time to send Americans into deep space, back to the moon and on to Mars.

Bush started his argument, as had politicians since JFK, with appeals to the past.

"Two centuries ago, Meriwether Lewis and William Clark left St. Louis to explore the new lands acquired in the Louisiana Purchase. They made that journey in the spirit of discovery to learn the potential of the vast new territory and to chart the way for others to follow.

"America has ventured forth into space for the same reasons. We've undertaken space travel because the desire to explore and understand is part of our character. And that quest has brought tangible benefits that improve our lives in countless ways."

What benefits were those? President Bush was pleased to explain.

"The exploration of space has led to advances in weather forecasting, in communications, in computing, search and rescue technology, robotics and electronics.

"Our investment in space exploration helped to create our satellite telecommunications network and the Global Positioning System.

"Medical technologies that help prolong life, such as the imaging processing used in CAT scanners and MRI machines, trace their origins to technology engineered for the use in space."

The argument for space exploration as a vehicle for technological development has always been a tried and true one. Bush had numerous examples to draw on. Going back to the moon and on to Mars would generate more such technology for the betterment of humankind.

Bush added a new argument for going back to the moon, related to the ultimate goal of sending astronauts to Mars.

"Returning to the moon is an important step for our space program. Establishing an extended human presence on the moon could vastly reduce the cost of further space exploration, making possible ever more ambitious missions.

"Lifting heavy spacecraft and fuel out of the Earth's gravity is expensive.

"Spacecraft assembled and provisioned on the moon could escape its far-lower gravity using far less energy and thus far less cost.

"Also, the moon is home to abundant resources. Its soil contains raw materials that might be harvested and processed into rocket fuel or breathable air.

"We can use our time on the moon to develop and test new approaches and technologies and systems that will allow us to function in other, more challenging, environments.

"The moon is a logical step toward further progress and achievement."

Bush later repeated the rationale for technology development, and resources. He added education and inspiration of the young, reasons that came naturally for a man who described himself as the "education president."

"And along this journey, we'll make many technological breakthroughs. We don't know yet what those breakthroughs will be. But we can be certain they'll come and that our efforts will be repaid many times over.

"We may discover resources on the moon or Mars that will boggle the imagination, that will test our limits to dream.

"And the fascination generated by further exploration will inspire our young people to study math and science and engineering and create a new generation of innovators and pioneers."

President Bush 43 proposed his version of a deep space exploration program with certain advantages that Bush 41 lacked.

First, in 1989, the space station program was in the design phase and was already suffering cost overruns and schedule slippages. Moreover, the space station was under attack by certain members of Congress, a coalition of liberal Democrats who opposed big, expensive space projects that spent money they felt better allocated to social programs, and a few conservative budget hawks who disliked spending of any kind. The Space Exploration Initiative was seen as a distraction from the space station, even by some inside NASA.

By 2004, the political fight over the space station had long concluded, and the orbiting lab was under construction with crews already engaged in research and development. Policy makers were already looking ahead to the next great space thing.

Second, Bush 43 had avoided one crucial mistake made by his father and had consulted the people who would implement the plan at NASA and pay for it in Congress. The arguments he made during his NASA Headquarters speech had already been tested to meet the approval of these stakeholders.

Finally. Bush was able to convince the stakeholders that his deep space program would be accomplished with less than a half a trillion over 20 to 30 years. Bush proposed winding down the space shuttle program after completion of the International Space Station and replacing it with a combination of commercial spacecraft and a new spaceship known as the Orion, which would be a 21st century version of the Apollo capsule, capable of missions to low Earth orbit and at least as far as the moon.

Unlike President Kennedy and the elder President Bush, Bush 43 did not mention what came to be known as the Vision for Space Exploration again. Selling the program fell first to NASA Administrator Sean O'Keefe and his successor, Mike Griffin.

Even before becoming NASA Administrator, Griffin, who had been involved in the Bush 41 Space Exploration Initiative, was a warm supporter of going back to the moon and on to Mars. However, according to a piece in *The Space Review*,[xii] Griffin had a slightly different rationale for a deep space exploration program.

"Griffin addressed the question of why the US should fund human space exploration. He dismissed the 'politically correct' answers of things like spinoffs and educational benefits in favor of a broader rationale. 'What the U.S. gains from a robust, focused program of human space exploration is the opportunity to carry the principles and values of western philosophy and culture along with the inevitable outward migration of humanity into the solar system,' he said. Such an effort, he noted, would be similar to the influence the British Empire had because of its mastery of the seas. 'Can America, through its mastery of human space flight, have a similar influence on the cultures and societies of the future, those yet to evolve in the solar system as well as those here on Earth? I think so, and I think our descendants will consider it to have been worth twenty cents per day.'"

The answer had a certain appeal for those people who still appreciated American nationalism and the primacy of western civilization. Modern audiences, especially those in the millennial generation, would no doubt be triggered by what Griffin had to say because of a certain disdain for those things. Others might wonder what potential international partners might think of Griffin's appeal to American exceptionalism.

The Vision for Space Exploration, in due course, failed for reasons I again set out in "Why Is It So Hard to Go Back to the Moon?" The short answer is that President George W. Bush was succeeded by a president who was not impressed with any of the arguments for space exploration, in particular American exceptionalism. That fact and a number of other factors doomed the second attempt to send American astronauts on voyages of discovery beyond low Earth orbit.

Chapter 4 – Why President Barack Obama did not want to return to the moon

2010-2016

On April 15, 2010, President Barack Obama entered the auditorium at the Kennedy Space Center keenly aware that he had a mess to clean up. A few months before, the OMB budget proposal had mandated that the Vision for Space Exploration that had been the centerpiece of President George W. Bush's space policy would be cancelled. Instead, the space agency would conduct a series of studies for a new heavy lift vehicle, deep space propulsion, and other "game changing" technologies that, in the fullness of time, might lead to a new and improved deep space exploration program.

The proposal had been met with bi-partisan fury from Congress and even in some corners of the media, usually friendly to the first African American president of the United States. The thoughts that were passing through Obama's mind as he walked up to the podium will likely never be known. Perhaps he was inwardly cursing Lori Garver, his campaign space advisor whom he had put in the position of Deputy Administrator of NASA, for getting him into the mess by advising him to take this course of action. President Bill Clinton had deep-sixed President George H. W. Bush's Space Exploration with barely a whimper. The younger Bush's program had gone off the rails, beset with schedule slippages and cost overruns. What, in the name of God, was the problem?

If Obama had been more introspective, he might have realized that his decision to end the Vision for Space Exploration was actually a break from Democratic space policy. President Jimmy Carter had saved the space shuttle program at a crucial time with an infusion of cash[xiii]. President Clinton had saved the space station from political oblivion with a redesign and by bringing in the Russians as full partners. Obama might have done the same with Bush 43's vision, making it his own. Indeed, the Second Augustine Commission had offered some recommendations along those lines.[xiv] Obama had largely ignored those recommendations.

The rank and file at NASA had been the most furious of all. It was bad enough that the end of the space shuttle program was going to cut employment at the space agency. No more deep space exploration was a punch to the gut. Obama's aides made sure that the people in the auditorium about to hear his speech did not include anyone who might want to heckle him.

Water under the bridge, as the saying goes. It was time to offer Plan B and see if it would quiet the critics.

In essence, Obama proposed a two-step deep space exploration program[xv]. First, American astronauts would travel to rendezvous with an Earth-approaching asteroid. These are rocks that hurtle in orbits around the sun, occasionally intersecting with the Earth's orbit. One such asteroid, 65 million years ago, crashed into the Earth in the vicinity of the Yucatan and killed the dinosaurs. Some visionaries dreamed of mining some of these asteroids and using the material to start space-based industries.

Then, Obama revealed the grand vision of his revamped space policy. "By the mid-2030s, I believe we can send humans to orbit Mars and return them safely to Earth. And a landing on Mars will follow. And I expect to be around to see it."

The plan sounded great. But many people in attendance or who heard about the speech later noticed something missing. Obama was quick to address the missing portion of his space plan.

"Now, I understand that some believe that we should attempt a return to the surface of the moon first, as previously planned. But I just have to say pretty bluntly here: We've been there before. Buzz has been there. There's a lot more of space to explore, and a lot more to learn when we do. So, I believe it's more important to ramp up our capabilities to reach -- and operate at -- a series of increasingly demanding targets, while advancing our technological capabilities with each step forward. And that's what this strategy does. And that's how we will ensure that our leadership in space is even stronger in this new century than it was in the last."

Buzz Aldrin was in the audience, having been brought to Florida aboard Air Force One as a political prop. Aldrin was and is a big supporter of sending humans to Mars. He thought that he was serving that cause by accompanying the commander in chief and lending his prestige as the second man to have walked on the moon to Obama's space plan. However, if Aldrin did not bury his face in his hands at the reason the president claimed that he did not want to send Americans to the moon, he must have felt like it. What Obama said did not make any sense whatsoever.

"Been there, done that" was one of the more transparently stupid reasons to bypass the moon. Human beings had explored small parts of Earth's nearest neighbor six time around the near side equatorial region. Much of the moon remained untrodden by human beings, especially the poles, where satellite probes had detected water ice in permanently shadowed craters.

The water is the key for returning to the moon. A study by MIT released three and a half years later suggested that using the moon as a refueling stop, as water can be broken down into oxygen and hydrogen, components of rocket fuel, would greatly decrease the weight and complexity of a human Mars mission.[xvi]

Even before the MIT study, space policy experts had speculated on the use of lunar water to not only sustain a settlement but to make rocket fuel. Lori Garver, while a political zealot, knows quite a bit about space policy, so she likely knew the singular value of lunar water. Did she inform the president of this fact? If so, he likely did not care.

When the stated reason for a policy decision is demonstrably ridiculous, usually a hidden reason exists. So, must it be with Obama specifically mocking the idea of returning to the moon.

The real reason for Obama's not wanting to return to the moon may reside in his disdain for the concept of American exceptionalism, the idea that the United States is a uniquely exceptional country among all other nations. As the Heritage Foundation pointed out, on a tour of European countries undertaken 2009, Obama quipped, "I believe in American exceptionalism, just as I suspect that the Brits believe in British exceptionalism and the Greeks believe in Greek exceptionalism."[xvii]

What does that mocking of American exceptionalism have to do with returning to the moon? Nothing illustrates the concept better than the sight of American astronauts walking and working on the moon. Obama wanted to avoid reminding Americans how exceptional they could be. He believed that the country that he was elected twice to govern had gotten too prideful for its own good and needed taking down a peg.

But one might respond, wouldn't American astronauts on Mars be an even greater reminder of American exceptionalism?

The question presupposes that Obama was serious when he proposed what NASA soon called the Journey to Mars. More likely the Mars mission proposal was a bright, shiny object meant as a distraction. People would not even orbit Mars for 23 years after 2010 when Obama proposed it. The landing date was deliberately left unsaid.

Further proof that the Journey to Mars plan that Obama proposed was not altogether serious occurred when the asteroid mission started to be downsized. The epic voyage to an Earth-approaching asteroid in short order became a mission to snatch a small asteroid with a robot probe and move it to lunar orbit for further visit by human astronauts. Then the plan devolved further to snatching a boulder off of the surface of an asteroid instead of moving the whole asteroid. The small bodies (asteroids and comets) science community rolled its collective eyes at the incredibly shrinking asteroid mission.

Richard Binzel of MIT put it best, calling the Asteroid Redirect Mission, as the project came to be called, "the emperor with no clothes, or at best with very thin cloth."[xviii]

None of that mattered. Besides, Obama may have known that space projects proposed by one president were often cancelled by the next president. He would have been right, but perhaps not in the way he may have expected.

Chapter 5 – Why Newt Gingrich wanted a moon base and why Mitt Romney said it was silly

2012

One of the great what-ifs of the 2012 campaign for the presidency concerns the candidacy of Newt Gingrich, former Speaker of the House, former history professor, and font of a myriad of ideas, some beyond the cutting edge, many outside the box, but all very interesting. Many of Gingrich's fans looked forward to a general election battle between Gingrich and then President Barack Obama in the same way that science fiction fans anticipated a clash between Obi Wan Kenobi and Darth Vader.

Alas, that epic battle never happened. The reason was, irony of ironies, one of Gingrich's better ideas, the establishment of a lunar settlement.

By the time Gingrich had decided to run for president he was already a well-known fixture in politics and the media. He had run twice for a House seat in Georgia before winning the third time he had run in 1978. Gingrich and a small band of Republican rebels had used the special orders time during House sessions, when members could make speeches about topics of their choosing, to attack the Democratic majority and advance conservative ideas.

Gingrich was most famous for executing a Republican takeover of the House and the Senate in 1994 using a list of promises known as the Contract With America. His four-year term as Speaker of the House was tumultuous, to put it mildly, but also productive. Gingrich was able to negotiate budget deals with then President Bill Clinton that led to the first budget surpluses in decades.

The former academic was always interested in space exploration as a way to transform American civilization. Gingrich had devoted a chapter of a book he published in the mid-1980s entitled "Window of Opportunity" to his musings about how much better history would have turned out if NASA had been allowed to pursue space exploration at the same level of spending as during the Apollo program.

I first encountered Gingrich during a Space Development Conference that took place in Houston in 1983. The then back bencher addressed the attendees with a proposal to build a solar power satellite, a facility that gathers sunlight from space and beams the power to Earth, as a "national project." I remember being fascinated that a member of Congress would think that way, though I also suspected that the world would never hear of Newt Gingrich again.

How was I to know?

The idea of a moon base came up during a December 10, 2011 debate in Iowa in advance of that state's caucuses. Mitt Romney, then a former governor of Massachusetts, was asked to explain what issues he disagreed with Gingrich about. Gingrich at the time had surged to the top of the polls. According to Space.com, Romney had a quick answer.[xix]

"Let's see. We can start with his idea to have a lunar colony that would mine minerals from the moon. I'm not in favor of spending that kind of money to do that."

Gingrich was quick to respond, using the tried and true education and inspiring the young argument.

"I'm proud of trying to find things that give young people a reason to study science and math and technology and telling them that some day in their lifetime, they could dream of going to the moon, they could dream of going to Mars,"

It should be noted that by that time, Gingrich was not proposing a revival of the Bush 41 Space Exploration Initiative or the Bush 43 Vision for Space Exploration. He had become a fervent critic of NASA bureaucracy which, in his view, impeded American progress in space. He favored building the moon base as a commercial venture, with government providing incentives in the form of prizes. The beauty of the prize approach was that government money would not be spent until a commercial company set up the moon base. The drawback was that the American federal government was pretty bad at setting aside money and leaving it alone for the years it would take to accomplish the object of the prize.

Gingrich would eventually come in fourth in the Iowa Caucuses. Undeterred, he gave a speech on space policy at a townhall meeting that took place in Cocoa Beach, Florida on January 25, 2012.[xx] The address was wide ranging, with references to President Abraham Lincoln, the Transcontinental Railroad, and the Wright Brothers.

After a while, Gingrich referred to how Romney was making fun of his idea for going back to the moon and noted an even wilder idea that he once proposed.

"I'm giving this background for our friends in the news media because twice recently Governor Romney has made fun of me for having bold ideas in space and has suggested that the idea of having a permanent lunar colony – he actually didn't catch the weirdest thing I've ever done and I'm going to tell you all because sooner or later his researchers will find it – at one point early in my career I introduced the Northwest Ordinance for Space, and I said when we get – I think the number was 13,000 – when we have 13,000 Americans living on the Moon they can petition to become a state."

Of course, there was method to Gingrich's madness. He went on to touch back on the inspiring the young argument,

"And here's the difference between romantics and so-called practical people. I wanted every young American to say to themselves: I could be one of those 13,000. I could be a pioneer. I need to study science and math and engineering. I need to learn how to be a technician. I can be part of building a bigger, better future. I can actually go out and live the future looking at the solar system and being part of a generation of courageous people who do something big and bold and heroic."

Gingrich's proposal of an American state on the moon, which likely would have run counter to the Outer Space Treaty, was part of an even greater vision of incorporating space into the American economic sphere.

"And here's the difference between romantics and so-called practical people. I wanted every young American to say to themselves: I could be one of those 13,000. I could be a pioneer. I need to study science and math and engineering. I need to learn how to be a technician. I can be part of building a bigger, better future. I can actually go out and live the future, looking at the solar system and being part of a generation of courageous people who do something big and bold and heroic."

Gingrich advanced both the economic argument and the argument for enhancing American power into his space vision, centered around settling the moon. He also discussed building propulsion technology that could get Americans to Mars, ramping up the frequency of rocket launches, and, ironically, cutting NASA's budget. The amount of money saved would go to prizes.

The unsaid reason for Gingrich's moon base proposal, and why he made it in Florida, stemmed from the fact that by 2012 Florida's space coast had gone into the economic doldrums, thanks to President Barack Obama's cancellation of the Bush 43 deep space exploration program. The transparent strategy was to win the Florida primary with the votes of displaced space workers, thus, hopefully, propelling Gingrich to winning the Republican nomination.

Alas, it was not to be. The very next day, during a debate in Jacksonville, Florida, Mitt Romney pounced, according to CBS News.[xxi]

"I spent 25 years in business. If I had a business executive come to me and say they wanted to spend a few hundred billion dollars to put a colony on the moon, I'd say, 'You're fired. The idea that corporate America wants to go off to the moon and build a colony there, it may be a big idea, but it's not a good idea."

Despite Gingrich's protestations, the statement had the effect on his campaign of a pin puncturing a balloon. The media, which had hitherto been neutral about Gingrich's moon base plan, became hostile. The plan was even a subject of a Saturday Night Live skit. Gingrich's campaign for president never recovered.

Ironically, as NASA Watch's Keith Cowing noted[xxii], Romney's space brain trust included a lot of back-to-the-moon supporters, including former NASA Administrator Mike Griffin, Gene Cernan, the last man to walk on the moon, and other space policy luminaries such as Scott Pace and Mark Albrecht. That fact suggests that privately Romney did not think that returning to the moon was such a crazy idea at all. Indeed, it had been policy during the Bush 43 administration. Had Romney been elected, we might have seen a revival of a NASA-centric deep space exploration program. If he had been asked about it, Romney might have responded that consistency is the hobgoblin of small minds.

Romney lost the 2012 election. Years later, Gingrich got the last laugh. As I noted in The Hill newspaper[xxiii], then governor of Florida and candidate for President in the 2016 elections, Jeb Bush pronounced Gingrich's moon base idea as "pretty cool."

The "coolness factor" has always been something that space exploration, including returning to the moon, had going for it. As it turned out, the eventual winner of the presidency in 2016 concluded that going back to the moon and on to Mars was "pretty cool" too.

Chapter 6 – President Donald Trump heads to the Moon, Mars and Beyond

2016-2017

Donald Trump has been, if nothing else, one of the most colorful and unusual people ever to occupy the office of president of the United States. He had spent most of his life as a real estate developer and then reality show host, not having climbed up the greasy pole of politics before he decided to run for president in 2015.

Until that time, Trump was more likely to grace tabloid gossip columns than the weightier space of more respectable newspapers. His various marriages and more casual relationships were constant fodder for celebrity talk.

Trump contemplated running for president as early as the beginning of the 21st century. His entry into politics had the air of Alexander the Great wondering if there were no more worlds to conquer. He had established himself in business and then media. Why not electoral politics?

Trump's approach to campaigning for president was unique in the history of the United States. He would offer his opponents and the media crude insults. He would give them ugly nicknames ("Lying Ted" and "Little Marco.") He would make outrageous accusations, such as the time he suggested that Senator Ted Cruz's father had been involved in the conspiracy to kill President Kennedy. The effect was to keep his opponents off balance.

Trump's policy proposals were a combination of economic nationalism, especially with regard to trade, good, old-fashioned Reagan-style tax and regulation cuts, and a winding down of a variety of foreign wars that Obama and Bush 43 had instigated more like a liberal Democrat than someone running on the Republican ticket. Most importantly, he spoke to tens of millions of Americans who felt abused by the political class of both parties. He would be the instrument of the people to put that political class in its place.

The strategy worked, despite the before-mentioned tabloid lifestyle that rose up to bite Trump when the Access Hollywood tape surfaced that had the candidate boasting about how he could get away with molesting women. Trump won because he pursued an electoral state strategy, unlike his opponent, the thoroughly unlikeable Hillary Clinton. He won a majority of the electoral votes but came in second behind Hillary in the popular vote.

Trump has governed a country that is deeply divided between people who adore him and people who positively loathe him. He has weathered a number of media disinformation campaigns, two attempts at impeachment, and the rise of a "never Trumper" movement of former conservatives who found him so repellant that they would prefer to support anyone, even Joe Biden, rather than to suffer a second term. Trump has used the media, including Twitter, to give as good as he has gotten.

When President Trump decided to send America on a course to the moon, Mars and beyond, he did not announce that intention during a speech. Instead, Trump started what would become Project Artemis during a ceremony in the Oval Office when he signed Space Policy Directive 1[xxiv]. The key part of SPD-1 stated that the United States would:

"Lead an innovative and sustainable program of exploration with commercial and international partners to enable human expansion across the solar system and to bring back to Earth new knowledge and opportunities. Beginning with missions beyond low-Earth orbit, the United States will lead the return of humans to the Moon for long-term exploration and utilization, followed by human missions to Mars and other destinations."

That President Trump, who loves little more than addressing cheering crowds, choosing such a low-key venue to announce the third time America would try to return to the moon, not to mention go to Mars and beyond, was a little curious. He might have chosen to rent out Rice Stadium in Houston and do a JFK. It is possible that Trump wanted to keep the matter low-key in order to allow the arguments for going back to the moon and do the other things to speak for themselves.

Trump was not always keen on deep space exploration. Space Policy Online notes[xxv] that Trump had an encounter with a young man while on the campaign trail during the 2016 election cycle.

"Trump was holding a campaign rally at Winnacunnet High School in Hampton, New Hampshire when a young man who identified himself as a NASA Space Technology Research Fellow in a joint MIT-Harvard Medical School program asked about putting humans on Mars. He noted that Trump complains that the United States needs to have victories again, and in the aerospace industry 'one of our biggest victories was putting man on the Moon.'

"Trump agreed with that, but when the NASA Fellow continued with his question — what did Trump think about sending humans to Mars — Trump's opinion was displayed more by his body language and tone of voice than his words. Shrugging and grimacing, he replied —

"'Honestly, I think it's wonderful. I want to rebuild our infrastructure first. OK? I think it's wonderful.' He then looked into the audience while pointing at the questioner dismissively."

Clearly something changed in the two years since that encounter. But when and how?

At late as August 2016, *Ars Technica* noted that Trump did not seem to have a space policy[xxvi]. He did invite Eileen Collins, the first woman to command a space shuttle mission, to speak at the Republican National Convention that year and call for an expansion of the space program

Fast forward to November 2016. *Ars Technica* began to note[xxvii] some activity in the Trump space policy shop after the real estate tycoon and reality show host won, much to the surprise of many people, including his opponent, Hillary Clinton.

"After multiple discussions with insiders, here's the state of play as best as *Ars* can understand it as of Thursday morning. Following the lobbyist purge, Trump's space policy team is being led by Mark Albrecht, a long-time Republican space policy adviser and former executive secretary of the National Space Council, which last existed in 1992. This influential council served as a bridge between the nation's civil and military space activities, and one of Trump's clearly defined goals is to reinstate the council, which Pence would likely head.

"Aside from Pence and Albrecht, the other key player in Trump's transition team with regard to space policy is one of its six vice chairs, former Speaker of the House Newt Gingrich, who would likely seek to shake things up at the space agency. Perhaps the biggest question facing NASA and space policy, then, is whether Trump will go for an outsider's space policy in the mode of Gingrich, which seems consistent with the stated desire to "drain the swamp," or whether he will accede to the pressures of big business and inertia."

The article mentioned the name of Jim Bridenstine, then a member of Congress from Oklahoma who had just been elected to his third and, he promised, his final term as a possible Trump NASA Administrator. Bridenstine was a conservative Republican who had a keen interest in going back to the moon and in space commercialization.

The reestablishment of the National Space Council, last convened during the Bush 41 administration, preceded Trump signing the first Space Policy Direction. The Space Council was chaired by Vice President Mike Pence and comprised of a number of cabinet secretaries and agency heads whose government departments dealt with space policy. The reformation of the National Space Council was early proof that President Trump was serious about space policy and its role in American life.

The first meeting of the National Space Council took place at the National Air and Space Museum's Steven F. Udvar-Hazy Center[xxviii]. The result of the meeting indicated that the Trump administration was going to break from Obama-era space policy and redirect America's attention back to the moon. According to NASA, then space agency acting Administrator Robert Lightfoot stated:

"The vice president also announced a call for renewed U.S. leadership in space – with a recommendation to the president that NASA help lead and shape the way forward. Specifically, NASA has been directed to develop a plan for an innovative and sustainable program of exploration with commercial and international partners to enable human expansion across the solar system, returning humans to the Moon for long-term exploration and utilization, followed by human missions to Mars and other destinations."

"American leadership" has been a reoccurring rationale for pursuing space exploration such as the exploration of the moon since the Kennedy Administration. The concept has been seen as an inherent good, something that should be promoted to secure the United States' position as a superpower.

The White House signing ceremony was attended by representatives of NASA's past and present, including Apollo moonwalkers Buzz Aldrin and Harrison Schmitt and space station astronauts Peggy Whitson and Christina Koch. Aldrin had found a new commander in chief and a new space plan to get behind, an experience that he doubtlessly hoped would not wind up with embarrassment.

Mike Pence summed up the day's proceedings. "Under President Trump's leadership, America will lead in space once again on all fronts. As the President has said, space is the 'next great American frontier' – and it is our duty – and our destiny – to settle that frontier with American leadership, courage, and values. The signing of this new directive is yet another promise kept by President Trump."

American leadership, courage, and values. Left unsaid but at the top of any mind who was paying attention, and not China's. Space races had become somewhat unpopular for many people. But the people who ran space policy for the Trump administration were well aware of the stakes for this latest attempt to jump-start an American-led deep space effort. The country that succeeded would own the future.

Robert Lightfoot added his thoughts. "NASA looks forward to supporting the president's directive strategically aligning our work to return humans to the Moon, travel to Mars and opening the deeper solar system beyond. This work represents a national effort on many fronts, with America leading the way. We will engage the best and brightest across government and private industry and our partners across the world to reach new milestones in human achievement. Our workforce is committed to this effort, and even now we are developing a flexible deep space infrastructure to support a steady cadence of increasingly complex missions that strengthens American leadership in the boundless frontier of space. The next generation will dream even bigger and reach higher as we launch challenging new missions and make new discoveries and technological breakthroughs on this dynamic path."

Again, the rationale of making scientific discoveries and creating new technology was trotted out. Would those and the other reasons be enough to sustain the United States' third attempt to go back to the moon and then beyond?

Lightfoot was only going to stick around until the new permanent NASA administrator was confirmed by the Senate. That process, usually pro forma, became a drama that was usually reserved for nominees for the Supreme Court, however.

Why did President Trump really change his mind and support a new effort to send Americans and allies beyond low Earth orbit? The answer may reside in the same reason Barack Obama opposed such an effort. Nothing speaks to American greatness more than space exploration. Trump's signature slogan was "Make America Great Again." The effort would include NASA and the nascent commercial space sector. So, Trump jumped into the effort with both feet. Thus, the personality of an unusual president met a historical moment to propel America, so it was hoped, back to the moon and beyond.

Chapter 7 – The Passion of Jim Bridenstine

2017-2019

Rep. Jim Bridenstine, R-Oklahoma, a 42-year-old former Navy aviator, sat at the witness chair for his confirmation hearing by the Senate Commerce Committee[xxix]. He already knew that he was in for some trouble because some of the Democratic members of the Committee had expressed opposition to his nomination. What followed, though, was a melodrama rarely seen in Washington. The nearly three hours of sheer hell that the Democratic senators put Bridenstine through was like a scene from an Allen Drury novel. Think of the hearings as *Advise and Consent Part 2: The Wrath of Bill Nelson*, and the gentle reader would not be far wrong[xxx].

Brindenstine was a rare nominee for NASA administrator in that he campaigned for the appointment. A year and a half before he sat in the lion's den of the Senate Commerce hearing room, he had introduced the American Space Renaissance Act[xxxi], a sweeping revision of space policy across the government that would affect the way that NASA, the military, and the commercial sector operated on the high frontier[xxxii].

The act itself was never meant to be passed in its original form but contained a variety of ideas that were designed to find their way into other authorization legislation. Ideas included giving the NASA Administrator a fixed five-year term, using the moon and cislunar space to accomplish a crewed mission to Mars, and a measure to promote space situational awareness.

On November 2, 2016, shortly before Donald Trump was elected president, Bridenstine addressed NASA's Lunar Exploration Analysis Group. He opened his mind about the moon's importance to ensuring American preeminence in space. He stated, "This is our Sputnik moment. America must forever be the preeminent spacefaring nation, and the Moon is our path to being so."

Bridenstine noted the discovery of water ice at the lunar poles. He noted its importance in transforming American commercial space. According to Space Policy Online[xxxiii]:

"He foresees a cis-lunar industry based on servicing and maintaining Earth-orbiting satellites that includes refueling those satellites using liquid oxygen and hydrogen produced from the Moon's water ice. If existing satellites can be refueled and otherwise maintained, fewer new spacecraft can be launched, reducing costs and the space debris population. He views the government's role as risk reduction to 'empower' commercial companies to establish such industries."

By the time that Trump assumed the presidency, Bridenstine had become a leading advocate for a return to the moon and the promotion of commercial space. Both of these facts caused me to endorse Bridenstine for the NASA administrator post[xxxiv]. Another factor spoke in favor of his appointment:

"Bridenstine would also bring together two warring factions that have divided the aerospace community. On one side are those like former NASA Administrator Mike Griffin, who prefer approaching space exploration from a traditional, Apollo-like method. On the other side are those, like Charles Miller of NextGenSpace, a member of the NASA transition team, who champion a more commercial approach. Because of his advocacy for commercial space, Bridenstine is a favorite of the commercial space faction. On the other hand, he advocates using the Orion spacecraft and the heavy-lift Space Launch System, which would make him acceptable to the Apollo redux faction. He suggests that other hardware, such as a lunar lander and surface habitats, should be acquired commercially, much in the same way as spacecraft are being acquired in the commercial crew program."

Bridenstine was also acquainted with Newt Gingrich, who was advising Trump on a variety of issues, including space policy. The then congressman was a political ally of Sen. Ted Cruz, R-Texas, who chaired the Senate subcommittee that oversees NASA. So, it was no surprise to anyone when Trump nominated Bridenstine just before Labor Day 2017.

At the time of his nomination, Bridenstine had already lived an interesting life. He had attended Rice University in Houston, taking an almost unprecedented triple major in business, psychology, and economics. He went on to get an MBA at Cornell.

Bridenstine flew an EC-2 Hawkeye aircraft as a naval aviator and later an F-18 at the Naval Strike and Air Warfare Center, the parent organization of Top Gun. He served a stint as the executive director of the Tulsa Air and Space Museum and Planetarium. At the time of his nomination to be administrator of NASA, Bridenstine was serving in his third term as a member of the United States House of Representatives.

Bridenstine's main antagonist, Sen. Bill Nelson, D-Florida, was a center-left politician who had spent decades climbing up the greasy pole of politics. He had served in the Florida House of Representatives, the United States House of Representatives, and, after a failed bid for governor of Florida, the office of Treasurer, Insurance Commissioner and Fire Marshal of Florida. Nelson was elected as a United States Senator in 2000 and was reelected comfortably twice.

As would be natural for a politician in a state that contains the Kennedy Space Center, Nelson had a keen interest in space policy. He parlayed that interest and his position in the House for a ride on a space shuttle *Columbia* mission in January 1986. Nelson encountered some resentment from NASA astronauts for the nakedly political means he had used to snatch a berth on the shuttle. His astronaut nickname was "ballast." His flight was the last successful shuttle mission before the *Challenger* disaster.

Nelson had opposed President Obama's cancellation of the Bush 43 Vision for Space Exploration. He remained a skeptic of commercial space, especially the Commercial Crew program. Nelson was a big booster of a humans to Mars program, largely because it would be of great benefit to constituents and campaign contributors located on Florida's space coast. He was also instrumental in getting the heavy lift Space Launch System started, a project criticized in many quarters as too expensive and competing with cheaper, commercial alternatives such as the SpaceX Starship.

The confirmation hearing lasted two and a half hours. Though they included three other, non-NASA nominees, the focus was almost entirely on Bridenstine. Nelson, during a long opening statement, offered the brief against the then congressman's confirmation. The core of the senator's argument was that Bridenstine, not being an "aerospace professional," was ill-equipped to make life and death decisions upon which the lives of astronauts would rely.

Nelson's argument was absurd on its face. Two of NASA's most celebrated administrators, James Webb and Sean O'Keefe, had come from non-technical backgrounds. Bridenstine himself pointed out that he would have talented engineers and scientists to advise him on such issues.

Committee Democrats also attacked Bridenstine on the issue of climate change. Climate change is a term used to describe what happens to the Earth's climate as more greenhouse gasses are pumped into the atmosphere, mainly from power plants and automobiles. Many on the Democratic side had taken the view that the fossil fuel industry had to be phased out entirely in favor of renewable (i.e. wind and solar) sources of power. They called people who dispute this approach or who suggested that climate change is not an existential threat to life on Earth "deniers." Thus, a scientific question had taken on the characteristic of a religious dispute.

Bridenstine, as a conservative congressman from an oil producing state, had spoken out against the idea of climate change being a threat. Thus, the committee Democrats labeled him as a "science denier." Science does not work like that. Theories are tested and altered all the time following experiments and new evidence.

Bridenstine conceded during the hearings that climate change exists, and humans likely have something to do with it. He pledged that as NASA administrator he would not interfere in the agency's scientific study of the phenomenon. But he reminded the committee that NASA would not set policy. The space agency would only provide information to those who do set policy.

Bridenstine did not escape criticism for positions he had taken that were seemingly unrelated to NASA's mission. For example, as a conservative Republican, he had expressed opposition to same-sex marriage. The same position had, at one time, been taken by President Barack Obama and Hillary Clinton. Nevertheless, the committee Democrats labeled him a homophobe, an unfair and false accusation.

The grilling that Bridenstine got caused one of the Republican members of the committee to ask the nominee, tongue in cheek. "Are you or have you ever been a conservative?" Eventually the committee reported the nomination out favorably along party lines. And then it remained stuck for several months.

The problem was that Bridenstine had ruffled some feathers among some members of the Republican senate caucus. He had supported a primary opponent to Sen. John McCain, R-Arizona. During the 2016 presidential campaign, Bidenstine, a supporter of Ted Cruz, had accused Sen Marco Rubio, R-Florida, of being soft on terrorism and illegal immigration. Both senators, in apparently pique, decided to retaliate by opposing Bridenstine's nomination. Sen. Jeff Flake, R-Arizona, also opposed the nomination, but only as a way to leverage concessions from the Republican Senate leadership.

There ensued a game of chicken between the Trump administration and Senator Nelson that lasted until April 2018. Neither side was willing to budge. Nelson, confident that he had won the argument, suggested that Trump choose another nominee more to his liking.

Bridenstine, clearly shaken by the abuse he endured during the hearings, suggested that Nelson thought that he was "some kind of jerk." In fact, to paraphrase a line from "The Godfather," Nelson regarded the fight as "not personal, strictly politics." The senator was a skeptic of returning to the moon and of commercial space. He was not prepared to accept a NASA administrator who disagreed with him on either issue.

Things came to a head in April 2018 when Robert Lightfoot announced that he would be stepping down as acting NASA Administrator. The decision sparked a crisis as no other person existed to fill that position.

At that point, Rubio, having gotten sufficiently over his hurt feelings from the 2016 campaign, switched his vote. Flake, having gotten satisfaction from the Republican senate leadership, did likewise. So, on April 19, 2018, the full Senate voted to confirm Jim Bridenstine as NASA administrator. Bridenstine proceeded to set about winning over some of his former critics, with some success, and getting NASA on course to returning to the moon.

As an ironic postscript, Bill Nelson went on to lose his bid for reelection to the Senate during the 2018 midterms. The result was a twist of Shakespearian dimensions. Having sought to wreck Jim Bridenstine's career, Nelson found his own political career in ruins.

The second twist occurred some months later. Bridenstine, when his confirmation was in doubt, had vowed to make Nelson his "best friend." The vow seemed to be quixotic at the time. However, rather than revel in the turn of events, Bridenstine offered Nelson a place on NASA's advisory committee. Nelson may have learned the bitter truth of "If you strike at the King, make sure you kill him," but he also experienced the grace of magnanimity at the hands of the man he sought to destroy. Thus, in service of the greater goal of sending humans back to the moon, Bidenstine proved to be a great statesman.

A third twist would occur after the Trump presidency completed and the Biden presidency began. More about that anon.

Chapter 8 – Elon Musk, the Coolest Capitalist of Them All

2002-2021

Elon Musk would be a remarkable character in a work of fiction. Born in apartheid-era South Africa, he immigrated first to Canada and then to the United States. After getting a degree in economics and physics at the University of Pennsylvania, he moved to California in 1995 at the height of the dot.com boom and started to make his first fortune.

Musk founded and then sold a series of companies, including PayPal, which he sold for $1.5 billion to eBay. Then he turned to his true passion, space travel, and founded a company called SpaceX in 2002. Within 18 years Musk was regularly flying satellites into space, had achieved the first privately crewed missions to the International Space Station, and had started to build and test an interplanetary spacecraft to fulfill his ultimate dream of founding a city on Mars. Incidentally, Musk had started a number of other enterprises, including an electric car company called Tesla and a rooftop solar power firm called Solar City.

Musk is no clean-limbed pure capitalist out of an Ayn Rand novel. For one thing, he is given to eccentric behavior, such as openly smoking weed on the Joe Rogan podcast. The incident elicited the wrath of Jim Bridenstine, who pointed out that such behavior was unseemly, not to mention illegal according to federal law, from an important government contractor.

Also, Musk was not shy about pursuing government contracts and incentives to enrich his various enterprises, something that a Hank Reardon would never dream of doing. The satellite launch market was filled with government customers such as the military and NASA. Musk also eagerly sought and got contracts to ship cargo and then people to the International Space Station under the Commercial Orbital Transportation Systems and Commercial Crew programs.

Musk is not afraid to hobnob with politicians who might prove useful. Early during the Obama presidency, he took the then president on a tour of the launch pad where his Falcon 9 sat ready to fly to the heavens. A few years later, Musk sat around a table with President Donald Trump to advise him on technology issues. Along the way he met with then Texas Governor Rick Perry to make the case that the Lone Star State should give SpaceX tax write offs and other incentives so that he might build a space port near the town of Boca Chica.

Yet Rand would have appreciated one thing about Elon Musk. The writer from Russia and the businessman from South Africa, both of whom prospered in the United States, had the same sorts of enemies. For example, Sen. Bernie Sanders. [xxxv]

"We can no longer tolerate a system that allows a billionaire like Elon Musk to gain $10.3 billion in one day, while 30 million unemployed workers are denied $600 a week to pay the rent and put food on the table. We need an economy that works for all, not just the 1%. #TaxTheRich"

Of course, anyone who understands economics, which is to say not Bernie, would point out that Musk's enterprises allowed quite a few people to pay the rent and put food on the table.

Elon Musk is the embodiment of a character that until he founded SpaceX lived only in fiction, that of the eccentric billionaire who started his own space program. Robert Heinlein created such a character named Delos Harriman in his "The Man Who Sold the Moon." He has also been compared to Tony Stark, the billionaire super hero in the Marvel Comics Universe.

Groups of people have been trying to start their own private rocket companies since the late 1970s, with little success. Space Services Inc. was one such company, founded by David Hannah, a real estate developer and friend of George H. W. Bush. The company, which at one time involved Mercury astronaut Deke Slayton, launched a number of in-house rockets with varying success. However, the company's first and only attempt to reach orbit failed on liftoff. The company was eventually bought out by L-3 Communications. It currently buys secondary payload space on other rockets for people who want their ashes launched into space.

Rotary Rocket Company was another attempt to create a private launch vehicle. The idea was to build a single-stage-to-orbit hybrid rocket/helicopter. The vehicle would fly initially with rotors powered by jets. Once the atmosphere was too thin for the rotors to work, rocket engines would kick in to take the vehicle the rest of the way to low Earth orbit. The landing process would be the reverse, with rockets slowing the descent most of the way to the ground and then the rotors slowing the vehicle the rest of the way. The company, plagued by design problems and a lack of money, folded in 2001.

Andrew Beal, a Dallas, Texas banker, formed Beal Aerospace with a goal of developing a privately funded heavy lift rocket. The BA-1 and the subsequent BA-2 were envisioned to service the communications satellite market. The launch vehicles used a unique engine design that used kerosene and a hydrogen peroxide oxidizer. Unfortunately, Beal could not find a market for its rockets and ceased commercial operations in the year 2000.

When Elon Musk started SpaceX in 2002 no one would have bet against the fledging company going the way of all the others. Indeed, the first three flights of its initial rocket, the Falcon 1 (named after Han Solo's Millennial Falcon), ended in failure. A fourth failure would likely have sunk the company.

However, the fourth launch of the Falcon 1 was a success, achieving low Earth orbit. The fifth and final launch carried a Malaysian satellite, SpaceX's first commercial customer. The flight was the last from the small launch vehicle. Musk and SpaceX had already moved on to the much larger Falcon 9.

The saga of the Falcon 1 demonstrated why SpaceX eventually succeeded where so many previous efforts failed. First, each launch failure was seen as a learning experience, with each destroyed rocket causing design changes that would be incorporated into newer models. The philosophy of test and then design would serve SpaceX well in subsequent years.

Also, Elon Musk proved to be just as good at marketing and getting other people to pay for his endeavor as he was at engineering. The first three Falcon 1 flights were paid for by DARPA. Flight 5 had a commercial customer.

However, the Falcon 9's development proved to be a result of the perfect convergence of opportunity, marketing, and engineering wizardry. The story starts a short time after SpaceX was founded, with an immense tragedy.

The disaster that led to the series of events that led to Elon Musk becoming the most successful commercial rocketeer in history started on February 1, 2003 when the space shuttle *Columbia* broke apart in the skies over Texas, killing its entire crew. The *Columbia* disaster led to nearly a year of soul searching at NASA and the Bush 43 administration that led to a new space policy that opened the door for commercial operators like Musk.

The Commercial Orbital Transportation System program was an initiative announced by NASA soon after President George W. Bush started the Vision for Space Exploration. The idea was a change for how NASA acquired Earth-to-low-Earth transportation services. Instead of acquiring such services in house (i.e. with the space shuttle) or with expensive cost-plus contracts with big aerospace firms, the space agency would acquire them with fixed priced contracts from the commercial sector. NASA would be a customer and not an owner of the vehicles thus developed and flown[xxxvi].

Thus, Musk got NASA to partly fund not only the Falcon 9 launch vehicle, but a spacecraft known as the Dragon. SpaceX won one of the contracts to take supplies to and from the International Space Station. After two test flights in 2010, SpaceX launched a Dragon in a successful test flight to the International Space Station on May 22, 2012. Thereafter, the Dragon made regular flights to and from the ISS. In the meantime, the Falcon 9 began launching commercial and military satellites, eventually becoming the most prolific launch vehicles in service.

Around this time. SpaceX started to add a unique feature to the Falcon 9, making the first stage reusable. Reusability had been the holy grail of spaceflight ever since the space shuttle was developed with that feature in mind. However, the time and cost it took to turn around the space shuttle orbiters after every flight negated much of the savings that reusability was expected to impart.

Musk's idea was for the first stage of the Falcon 9 to descend back to Earth after the second stage had separated. It would either land on a drone ship in the Atlantic Ocean or a landing pad near the launch site in Florida.

Over four years, SpaceX conducted tests of the Falcon 9 first stage, plunging some into the ocean in a controlled way, aiming for a drone ship later. The first successful landing of a Falcon 9 first stage occurred in December 2015 when it touched down at a landing pad in Florida. The first successful landing on a drone ship occurred in April 2016. SpaceX currently regularly lands the Falcon 9 first stage.

More importantly. SpaceX has learned to turn around and reuse the Falcon 9 first stage in a cost-effective manner. The ability has greatly reduced the launch cost of the Falcon 9 and has rendered every other launch system obsolete.

Musk was not content just to have a launch vehicle that could undercut every other rocket in existence on price. He also developed the first privately funded heavy lift rocket, called the Falcon Heavy. The Falcon Heavy consists of an augmented Falcon 9 core with two Falcon-9-derived strap-ons and a second stage. It is capable of lifting almost 64,000 kilograms to a geostationary transfer orbit and almost 17,000 kilograms to Mars. Falcon Heavy is designed for heavy communications satellites and interplanetary science missions.

The first launch of the Falcon Heavy took place on February 6, 2018. The usual practice when test-flying a new launch vehicle is to put up a dummy payload. Musk, ever the showman, launched a used Tesla Roadster electric car with a spacesuit-clad mannequin at the wheel, which he dubbed "Starman."

The launch was a complete success. The two strap-on boosters landed simultaneously on land. Unfortunately, the central core first stage missed the drone ship and crashed into the water.

The image of Starman at the wheel in the Tesla Roadster, with the Earth in the background, headed out into interplanetary space, captured the world's imagination. To date, Falcon Heavy has launched two more times, once with a commercial customer, once with a Defense Department payload. The number of commercial contracts SpaceX has signed has covered the development cost of the Falcon Heavy. The launch vehicle has been mentioned for support of the Project Artemis program to return to the moon.

Elon Musk and SpaceX are currently engaged in two potentially world-changing projects.

SpaceX is launching a constellation of satellites called Starlink[xxxvii] that is designed to bring internet communications to the entire planet. The project is somewhat controversial because the astronomy community has complained that the bright objects are interfering with ground-based observations. SpaceX is endeavoring to mitigate the problem. In any case, when the constellation is complete, Musk stands to make annual revenue of over $10 billion a year by 2025 from selling services from Starlink.

In the meantime, SpaceX is developing a huge, two-stage spacecraft at its facility in Boca Chica, Texas that is designed to take people and cargo to the moon, Mars, and beyond. The project has gone through a number of design and name changes, including Mars Colonial Transporter and Interplanetary Transport System. Currently the spacecraft's upper stage has been dubbed Starship and the lower stage Super Heavy.

The SpaceX facility at Boca Chica was originally sold as an alternate launch site for the Falcon 9 and Falcon Heavy. Instead, it has morphed into a test facility and potential future launch site for the Starship/Super Heavy rocket ship. The spacecraft, if and when it is finally operational, will be the largest, most powerful launch vehicle in history. It will be entirely reusable and capable of taking 100 tons to the moon and Mars, as well as other destinations in the Solar System.

The Starship is the vessel of Elon Musk's ultimate dream of founding a million-person city on Mars. The rocket is also envisioned to land on the moon. Indeed, NASA has included a derivative of the Starship as a competitor for a human lunar lander in the Project Artemis program.

Elon Musk is the most popular billionaire on the planet, irrespective of the ire that Bernie Sanders holds him in. He has shocked people on occasion with his eccentric behavior. NASA Administrator Jim Bridenstine was once obliged to remind him that he needed to pay attention to his Commercial Crew obligations with the space agency. Like President Trump, Musk occasionally gets into trouble on Twitter. But, largely because of his efforts to single-handedly open up the high frontier of space, he has become the coolest capitalist of all. Many expect SpaceX to land on the moon and Mars long before NASA manages it. Musk may well do so with NASA in the end.

Chapter 9 – To the Moon by 2024?

2019-2021

When President John F. Kennedy first proposed landing a man on the moon and returning him safely to the Earth, he set a deadline of "before this decade is out." The thing was accomplished with five months and a few days to spare.

Since then, attempts to return to the moon had less ambitious deadlines. President George H. W. Bush suggested the year 2000 as the year Americans return to the moon, some 11 years after he made the big announcement. President George W. Bush suggested 2020 as the big year of the lunar return, some 16 years after he made his proposal. Neither deadline was met because both efforts were cancelled literally before they got off the ground.

When President Trump signed the executive order launching Project Artemis and the third attempt to return to the moon, the deadline of 2028 was set. Once again, the lunar return would proceed at a relatively leisurely pace.

All of that changed when Vice President Mike Pence made a startling announcement in March 2019 during a meeting of the National Space Council. Now the first woman and the next man would land on the moon in 2024, just five years hence. Pence suggested that the United States was in a space race, not only with Russia, but with China. According to Space.com[xxxviii], the Vice President revealed a new reason for returning to the moon, echoing the motives for the Apollo race to the moon of the 1960s.

"Urgency must be our watchword. The United States must remain first in space in this century as in the last, not just to propel our economy and secure our nation but, above all, because the rules and values of space, like every great frontier, will be written by those who have the courage to get there first and the commitment to stay."

NASA Administrator Jim Bridenstine added his own arguments.

First, by bringing the date of the next moon landing forward four years, NASA would retire what he called "political risk." The idea was that the less time it takes to start people going back to the moon, the less time that politicians would have the opportunity to cancel the program out of a fit of ADD or because they consider it a cash cow for other priorities.

Second, the then five-years-hence deadline would concentrate the minds of NASA and contractor engineers. If the date was eight or nine years out, schedule slippages would seem to be less meaningful.

Finally, as Bridenstine pointed out, the cost of getting to the moon would be less if the timeline was five years. Less overhead and the ability to spend money on a curve rather than flattening the spending would make the program more efficient. Unfortunately, it also meant that the amount of spending per year would increase.

Not everyone had bought the plan to land on the moon in 2024. During a hearing before the House Appropriations subcommittee that funds NASA that took place in October 16, 2019, then subcommittee chair Rep. Jose Serrano, D-New York, was pretty sure about the real reason for the 2024 landing deadline, according to Space.com[xxxix].

"Since NASA has already programmed the lunar landing mission for 2028, why does it suddenly need to speed up the clock by four years, time that is needed to carry out a successful program from a science and safety perspective? To a lot of members, the motivation appears to be just a political one, giving President Trump a moon landing in a possible second term, should he be re-elected."

The fact that Serrano was in the position to make trouble for NASA as the man with the power to provide or withhold funding was an unfortunate effect of the 2018 midterm election, which flipped the House from Republican to Democratic control. Before 2018, Rep. John Culberson, R-Texas, was the subcommittee chair. Culberson was an enthusiastic supporter of NASA funding and doubtless would have greeted the 2024 deadline with more enthusiasm. He lost his seat to a Houston corporate attorney named Lizzie Fletcher in part because of that enthusiasm.

While no one has recorded an instance of Trump rubbing his hands together and grinning at the thought of concluding his hypothetical second term with a moon shot, Serrano was doubtless correct that the thought had crossed his mind. However, even if the moon shot takes place after the end of a second Trump term, he would doubtless be at the Kennedy Space Center to see the astronauts off and to take credit. Besides, that likelihood does not make the other reasons invalid.

It does not matter much whether Americans return to the moon in 2024 or 2025 or some later year, so long as they return. The purpose of the 2024 date is to signal that this time the United States is serious about returning to the moon, sooner rather than later.

In the end, two things occurred to make the 2024 moon landing all but impossible. First, Congress appropriated a smaller amount than the money NASA requested for the commercially acquired Human Landing System. Second, Donald Trump lost his bid for reelection at the hands of former Vice President Joe Biden.

Chapter 10 – How are we going to land on the moon?

2019-2021

When President Trump signed the executive order to return American astronauts to the moon, two mission elements, the heavy lift Space Launch System and the Orion spacecraft, had already been in development for several years. The fact had a good news/bad news aspect to it.

The good news was that NASA was not obliged to start from scratch. While over seven years after President Barack Obama had cancelled the Bush 43-era moon program, the United States Congress forced the administration to continue to fund the SLS and the Orion. The two pieces of space hardware were justified as part of Obama's "Journey to Mars" program, allegedly to send astronauts directly to the Red Planet and to examine a rock collected from an asteroid to be carried to lunar orbit by some means.

The bad news was that both the Orion and the SLS had proven to be horrendously expensive, suffering cost overruns and schedule slippages. They were examples of what often happened to large-scale space projects, operated on cost-plus contracts, during NASA's post-Apollo years.

Nevertheless, the two pieces of hardware were proceeding apace. The plan was to launch the Orion around the moon uncrewed in 2021, crewed in 2023, and then attempt the moon landing in 2024.

The last mission, dubbed Artemis III, was going to be a problem. As late as when Vice President Pence announced the 2024 landing date, a human-rated lunar lander was not in development.

NASA had already initiated a program called the Commercial Lunar Payload Services (CLPS) for robotic lunar landers. NASA planned to use the COTS and Commercial Crew model to solicit commercial companies to build and send lunar landers equipped with instruments from NASA and other vendors.

In May 2019, NASA awarded the first round of contracts. The commercial lunar lander companies were Astrobotic, Intuitive Machines, and Orbit Beyond. However, two months later, Orbit Beyond dropped out. In April 2020, NASA awarded Masten Space Systems a CLPS contract. The first commercial lunar lander was slated to land on the moon as early as 2021.

However, if NASA proposes to land humans on the moon, it will need landing systems many orders of magnitude larger and more capable than anything being developed under CLPS. Such landers must be rapidly developed and fully funded if the space agency is to have any hope of meeting the 2024 deadline.

In July 2019, NASA's Marshal Spaceflight Center was designated the lead developer of the Human Landing System. In October 2019 NASA sent out requests for proposals for developing the HLS. In April 2020, the space agency selected three teams, one led by SpaceX, one by Blue Origin, and the third by Dynetics. Conspicuously, a proposal by the venerable aerospace giant Boeing did not make the cut.

Selection of the three lunar lander candidates was bound up in Douglas Loverro's brief career as associate administrator of NASA's Human Exploration and Operations Mission Directorate. NASA Administrator Jim Bridenstine announced Loverro's selection on October 16, 2019.[xl]

Loverro's experience was impressive. "For three decades, Loverro was in the Department of Defense and the National Reconnaissance Office developing, managing, and establishing national policy for the full range of national security space activities."

Most of Loverro's recent experience was in the military side of space policy.

"From 2013 to 2017, Loverro served as the Deputy Assistant Secretary of Defense for Space Policy. In this role, he was responsible for establishing policy for the United States allies to the benefits of space capabilities and to help guide the department's strategy for addressing space-related issues. He led departmental activities in international space cooperation, assessment of the national security impacts of commercial space activities, and oversaw the establishment of a strategy for addressing growing challenges in space security."

Still. Loverro's ascent to become in charge of all of NASA's human space flight operations, including the International Space Station, the commercial crew program, and Artemis was met with great approval.

Therefore, space observers were surprised when less than seven months later, in May 2020, Loverro abruptly resigned.

Loverro was somewhat vague as to the reason for his resignation, only saying that he had made a "mistake" earlier in the year. What that mistake was, he decorously declined to say. However, some journalists, doing a little digging, uncovered an awful truth. Ars Technica relates[xli] the following story:

"He made an error during the procurement process of the Human Landing System, during which NASA selected bids from Blue Origin, Dynetics, and SpaceX to build lunar landers as part of the Artemis Program. In his resignation letter to employees on Tuesday, Loverro admitted he made a 'mistake' earlier this year. Multiple sources have suggested that he violated the Procurement Integrity Act."

The violation could be considered a criminal offense. But why would a seasoned aerospace professional do such a thing?

It seems that Loverro had reservations about the winning bids for the Human Lunar Lander. He preferred the Boeing lander and wanted to make sure that the proposal made the final cut.

"So Loverro was under the gun to get humans on the Moon by 2024, he had concerns about most of the bids, and he favored integrated launch. This means Loverro likely favored the design of Boeing's bid for a Human Landing System, which entailed launching an integrated lander on a 'commercial' Space Launch System rocket. It seems reasonable to assume that Loverro may have been pushing Boeing to come up with a more competitive bid. "

Loverro likely violated the law by giving the Boeing team inside information unavailable to the other competitors. And, apparently, the NASA Office of Inspector General found out.

Loverro's motives were pure in the sense that he believed that the Boeing design had the best chance of making the 2024 date for the next moon landing. However, as of this writing, a criminal investigation is ongoing.

The next wrinkle to touch on commercial human moon lander development occurred when the House subcommittee that oversees NASA passed its version of a space agency authorization bill, HR5666.[xlii] The bill reflected huge differences between subcommittee Democrats and NASA about how America should go back to the moon and why.

The bill would prohibit establishing a permanent lunar base and technology development that would use lunar resources to sustain astronauts exploring the moon. Most importantly, the bill demanded that the human moon lander would be "owned" by NASA and not commercial entities.

The restrictions on the bill derived from the Democrat members' desire to use the moon solely as a testing ground for eventual missions to Mars. Understandably, the bill received plenty of pushback from various stakeholders.

A group of concerned scientists posted their objections in a letter to Rep Bernice Johnson, chair of the House Science Committee, and Rep. Kendra Horn, chair of the subcommittee that passed the NASA authorization bill.[xliii]

"NASA has been given a set of restrictive instructions that will prevent sustainability and economic development from being built into our human space flight program. This is illustrated by the requirement for government ownership, and by implication, the traditional cost-plus contracting method for the Human Landing System. The way we interpret the bill means commercial involvement will be limited to the CLPS program that will not be allowed to grow beyond NASA contracts. As was shown by the Apollo program, a wholly taxpayer-funded human spaceflight program is not sustainable. Therefore, as we look to expand humanity to the Moon and beyond, it is critical that the American taxpayer be shown that there can be a tangible return on the investment of sending humans to survive and thrive off planet Earth.

"The terms of the bill are overly prescriptive. As written, human missions to the lunar surface are limited to a small number of sortie missions. These portions of the bill appear to have been written with the false perspective that the Moon has no intrinsic value as a destination and that its resources and experience gained operating there make no contribution to further Mars exploration activities. Our strong assertion is that the Moon is an enabling asset that will foster sustainable human exploration of Mars, while expanding the economic sphere of the United States and our international partners. Additionally, this development will produce tangible economic returns on taxpayer investment to society back on Earth."

The letter went on to criticize the bill as irrational, not only from the standpoint of the moon as a useful destination for science, commerce, and political soft power, but as a proving ground for later missions to Mars.

The Commercial Spaceflight Federation's reaction was terser but just as to the point.[xliv]

"As written, the NASA Authorization bill would not create a sustainable space exploration architecture and would instead set NASA up for failure by eliminating commercial participation and competition in key programs. As NASA and the White House have repeatedly stated, any sustainable space exploration effort must bring together the best of government and commercial industry to achieve a safe and affordable 21st century space enterprise. We look forward to working with members of the House Space Subcommittee to address a number of concerns with the bill."

NASA Administrator Jim Bridenstine's reaction was more nuanced but, in the end, just as blunt.[xlv] While he praised the committee for its "bipartisan" approach, he was forthright with his reasons why the bill, as then written, was not acceptable.

"I am concerned that the bill imposes some significant constraints on our approach to lunar exploration. As you know, NASA has successfully fostered the development of a rapidly expanding commercial economy for access to space. We would like to continue building on this success as we develop the most efficient mission architectures and partnership approaches to accomplish our shared goals.

"NASA seeks to expand the sphere of economic activity deeper into space by conducting space exploration and development with commercial and international partners. Without the dynamic participation of commercial partners, our chances of creating a sustainable exploration program are significantly diminished. In particular, we are concerned that the bill's approach to developing a human lander system as fully government-owned and directed would be ineffective. The approach established by the bill would inhibit our ability to develop a flexible architecture that takes advantage of the full array of national capabilities – government and private sector – to accomplish national goals. NASA would appreciate the opportunity to work with the Committee to develop language that would support a broader national and international effort that would maximize progress toward our shared exploration goals through the efficient application of our available resources."

Bridenstine went on to point out that the bill made no sense even in support of the Mars goal.

"NASA is fully committed to a lunar exploration program that supports and enables human missions to Mars. The Committee should be aware that the exploration of Mars is a very challenging goal both technically and from a resource perspective. If we are going to accomplish this goal, we will need the flexibility to rapidly develop technical expertise using the Moon and to fully engage commercial and international partners. We do think that the bill's concerns for limiting activities on the Moon could be counterproductive. If we are going to explore Mars in a safe and sustainable way, we will require a strong in situ resource utilization capability and significant technology development using the surface of the Moon. NASA would appreciate more flexibility in defining lunar surface activities that may contribute directly to Mars exploration."

The reaction from some of the media was just as harsh. Ars Technica suggested[xlvi] that the House NASA bill constituted a plot to hand NASA's human spaceflight program to Boeing, a company that had fallen short in recent months in aerospace performance but still had clout on Capitol Hill. Even further, the article suggested that the House panel had rejected the systematic, commercial-based approach to space exploration being put forth by the Trump administration in favor of a "flags and footsteps" program similar to the Apollo program.

HR5666 was not been voted on by the full committee. It was not passed by both houses of Congress in its current form nor signed into law by President Donald Trump. The legislation died with the end of the 116th Congress.

The spending bill that included NASA passed the House but not the Senate as the 2021 fiscal year began. The Trump Administration proposed a healthy 12 percent increase in the space agency's budget, including $3.3 billion for the Human Landing System. The House offered a flat NASA bill with just $628.3 million for the HLS. Under those numbers a moon landing in 2024 would be all but impossible to execute.

In the meantime, the Senate appropriations subcommittee that funds NASA seemed to be more favorable to providing full funding for the Human Landing System. However, Sen. Jerry Moran, chair of the Senate Appropriations Subcommittee on Commerce, Justice, Science, and Related Agencies stated[xlvii], "We will try to provide all the necessary funding to keep Artemis on track for a lunar landing on schedule, but it is and will remain a challenge."

In the end, the NASA spending bill that passed both houses of Congress contained just $850 million for the Human Landing System. The amount, while certainly better than nothing, was inadequate to achieve a human lunar landing by 2024. By the time the omnibus spending bill passed in December 2020, President Trump had lost his bid for reelection. The fate of the whole Artemis program remained in doubt with the ascent of Joe Biden to the presidency.

The back and forth over acquiring a means to land humans on the moon proves the adage that is common to large-scale government space projects. The technology is easy. The politics is hard.

Chapter 11 – The Artemis Accords

2020-2021

On October 13, 2020, eight nations signed an agreement known as the Artemis Accords[xlviii], which are meant to govern the exploration of space. The United States, the United Kingdom, the United Arab Emirates, Canada, Italy, Luxembourg, Australia, and Japan signed the agreement that touched on a number of areas that would, it is hoped, prevent conflict on the high frontier of space as human civilization expanded out from the confines of Earth.[xlix]

"The accords, seven pages long, outline a series of principles that countries participating in the Artemis program are expected to adhere to, from interoperability and release of scientific data to use of space resources and preserving space heritage. Many of the principles stem directly from the Outer Space Treaty and related treaties."

The signing was the result of several months of negotiation with various countries that were thought to be suitable partners for the Artemis return to the moon program. The idea behind the accords was that the Artemis program would be the beginning of a process that would involve open ended activities by human beings, first on the moon, then Mars and elsewhere. Nations that signed on to the Artemis Accords agreed to follow certain rules to promote peace and mutual cooperation.

While the Artemis Accords seem to be a sensible mechanism to govern the peaceful exploration and commercial development of space, support for them is not universal.

For example, Christopher Newman, a professor of Space Law and Policy at Northumbria University, Newcastle in the U.K., suggested that a number of countries are reluctant to sign the Artemis Accords.[l] The reason seems to be processed based rather than the contents of the Accords, which Professor Newman finds to be noncontroversial.

"If the substance is reassuring, the US promotion of the accords outside of the 'normal' channels of international space law – such as the UN Committee on the Peaceful Uses of Outer Space – will be a cause of consternation for some states. By requiring potential collaborators to sign bilateral agreements on behavior instead, some nations will see the US as trying to impose their own quasi-legal rules. This could see the US leveraging partnership agreements and lucrative financial contracts to reinforce its own dominant leadership position."

Even the casual reader might react by crying out "duh!" The Artemis Program is an American initiative. It is only natural that the United States is seeking a leadership position.

Russia, whose relations with the United States have chilled under Vladimir Putin, is resisting joining the Artemis Accords. China, which has become an outright hostile power to the West, especially in the wake of the Coronavirus, is not a candidate for the Artemis Accords.

But what about other, nominally friendly nations? Professor Newman has an explanation.

"Intriguingly Germany, France and India are also absent. These are countries with well developed space programs that would surely have benefited from being involved in Project

Artemis. Their opposition may be down to a preference for the moon Agreement and a desire to see a properly negotiated treaty governing lunar exploration."

The "moon agreement" that Newman references is likely the Moon Treaty that was drawn up in the late 1970s and was rejected by the United States because of its severe restrictions on commercial space development, especially resource extraction. Expert opinion suggests that these and other countries were come around because the logic of being a partner in the Artemis Program far outweighs clinging to an outdated treaty whose assumptions are obsolete with the rise of the commercial space sector.

Even so, Stephen Buono, a postdoctoral fellow at Stanford University's Center for International Security and Cooperation, has similar process-oriented objections to the Artemis Accords, published in the Hill.[li] Buono believes that the development of space law needs to be the purview of the UN's Committee on the Peaceful Uses of Outer Space. NASA and the United States setting up a regime on its own smacks of unilateralism, in Buono's view. Also, he has another objection.

"Artemis-based law is also dangerous. Each independent step the United States takes toward commercializing the Moon's resources is one taken away from important potential partners in space, as well as rivals worth keeping in the loop. These include dozens of nations in the developing world who consider lunar resources the common property of all people, and Russia and China, two massive spacefaring powers whose participation in international space law is indispensable to its legitimacy. It is with Russia and China, too, who American mining interests must reckon — whether or not these U.S. rivals join the Artemis fold."

In other words, the United States should accept the provisions of the Moon Treaty which it rejected 40 years ago and only one independent space power, India, is a party to. The idea is absurd on its face. The idea that developing world countries, not to speak of hostile powers such as Russia and China, should have veto power over what the United States and the other parties of the Artemis Accords should do on the moon or anywhere else is laughable.

Besides, the fact that an entity has ownership of resources extracted from a celestial body such as the moon has already been established. No nation disputes that the United States owns the moon rocks that the Apollo astronauts collected from the lunar surface decades ago. The precedent has been established for other countries and for private entities.

The Artemis Accords are an attempt to prevent conflict in space over resources by establishing rules and protocols about how they should be extracted. If a hostile power were to attempt to interfere with such operations, it would be considered an act of war. No sensible government would go to war over extraterrestrial resources when an agreement is ready to be signed that regulates their extraction in a peaceful, equitable manner.

In conclusion, the Artemis Accords are a work in progress[lii]. It not only needs to have new signatories to become effective as a governing document but also has to survive a change of American administrations. It does not have the force of a treaty, so any agreement crafted by one president can be summarily repudiated by another, though the consequences in lost prestige and embarrassment would be severe.

Trump is out, Biden is in, Now what?

Chapter 12: Why does Joe Biden want to go back to the moon?

2020-2021

Election 2020 turned out to be one of the weirdest presidential elections in recent American history. President Trump built on his 2016 vote total to win over 74 million votes. However, former Vice President Joe Biden won about 80 million votes and handily beat the president in both the popular and electoral vote totals.

President Trump's ill-considered campaign to overthrow the results of the 2020 election in the courts will, no doubt, be studied by historians for generations. Trump's tendency to take things long past the boundaries of reason had served him well in business and in politics. However, this time, his campaign to snatch victory out of the jaws of defeat earned him an unprecedented second impeachment and an occupation of the Capitol Building that was at once a comic opera and dangerous incident.

Regardless of Trump's efforts, Joe Biden was sworn in as president of the United States behind protective fencing and under the guns of 25,000 or so National Guardsmen. Donald Trump retreated to Mar-A-Largo to plot his next move and to fend off mounting legal assaults on issues dating back decades.

Why did Trump lose? The reason seems to be a combination of the 45th president's acerbic behavior and the effects of the coronavirus pandemic. The pandemic, which came out of China to ravage the world, hit the United States with a force not seen since the Spanish Flu Pandemic of a century before. Americans were obliged to hunker down at home, wear face masks while out, and otherwise practice measures to slow the spread of the pandemic. The economy, which had been roaring before thanks to Trump's approach of low taxes, deregulation, and a hard line on illegal immigration and foreign trade, went into a tailspin. The president's enemies gleefully blamed him for the ill effects of the pandemic. Ironically, thanks to Operation Warp Speed, the Trump administration enabled the development of effective vaccines against the coronavirus, which started to be distributed shortly before the end of the Trump presidency.

One issue that had not been a bone of contention during the general election campaign was the Artemis program. Trump would occasionally tout the return to the moon and on to Mars project during campaign speeches. However, Biden, when he would campaign at all, did not mention NASA's signature undertaking.

However, the Democratic Platform for 2020 endorsed the Artemis program.[liii] Tucked in toward the end of the section "Investing in the Engines of Job Creation" was the following sentence:

"We support NASA's work to return Americans to the moon and go beyond to Mars, taking the next step in exploring our solar system."

Still, people forecasting what a Biden space policy would look like were only guessing. The very first thing that Team Biden did regarding NASA was to choose a transition team whose job it was to exam the state of the space agency and to offer recommendations to the incoming administration. According to Space.com[liv] the members of the team consisted primarily of scientists and other academics and was led by former astronaut Ellen Stofan. One exception was Dave Nobel, an official of the ACLU, an expert in diversity hiring, though he also worked as "White House liaison and deputy chief of staff at NASA."

Notable for an absence on the team was any high-profile politician or former high ranking NASA official. The makeup of the team did not offer many clues as to what Biden's space policy was likely to be. Reading the tea leaves, Space News suggested that climate change would achieve some level of importance at NASA over space exploration[lv]. The supposition made sense. Biden had adopted climate change as one of his signature issues during the campaign, topped only by the coronavirus pandemic.

Biden's method of governing once he was sworn into office did not give supporters of the Artemis program much comfort. He was prolific in the number of executive orders he signed that overturned a great many Trump priorities, ranging from the Keystone XL pipeline to illegal immigration enforcement. Since Artemis was also a Trump priority, would Biden get around to cancelling it, much as Obama had cancelled the Constellation program and Clinton the Space Exploration Initiative?

Artemis' chief advocate, NASA Administrator Jim Bridenstine, had announced that he would resign should Biden be elected, the idea being that the new president would need to choose someone he could truth for the position. The day Biden was sworn in, Bridenstine duly tendered his resignation. The development was met with mourning across the political spectrum. Bridenstine had gone a long way since his confirmation hearing when he was the subject of calumnies by senate Democrats. He was admired on both sides of the aisle.

Soon after his resignation, Bridenstine moved back to Oklahoma and took a job with a private equity firm. After nearly ten years of public service, first as a member of Congress then as NASA administrator, he got a chance to get reacquainted with his family and to make a little money. But his change of career meant that Bridenstine was not available to campaign for the continuation of Artemis with the new administration.

Back in July 2019 former NASA Deputy Administrator Lori Garver offered an alternate vision for NASA that eschewed space exploration in favor of fighting climate change[lvi]. She claimed that there was no public appetite for space exploration but plenty of support for fighting climate change.

"The public is right about this. Climate change — not Russia, much less China — is today's existential threat. Data from NASA satellites show that future generations here on Earth will suffer from food and water shortages, increased disease and conflict over diminished resources. In 2018, the National Academy of Sciences released its decadal survey for Earth science and declared that NASA should prioritize the study of the global hydrological cycle; distribution and movement of mass between oceans, ice sheets, ground water and atmosphere; and changes in surface biology and geology. Immediately developing these sensors and satellites while extending existing missions would increase the cadence of new, more precise measurements and contribute to critical, higher-fidelity climate models."

NASA has always had a vigorous Earth Science program, largely involved in launching Earth observation satellites. Garver wanted to go further than that,

"NASA could also move beyond measurement and into action — focusing on solutions for communities at the front lines of drought, flooding and heat extremes. It could develop and disseminate standardized applications that provide actionable information to populations that are the most vulnerable. NASA could create a Climate Corps — modeled after the Peace Corps — in which scientists and engineers spend two years in local communities understanding the unique challenges they face, training local populations and connecting them with the data and science needed to support smart, local decision-making."

It should be noted that by the time the article came out, Gatver had founded an organization called the Earthrise Alliance[lvii], the purpose of which was to convert Earth observation data into easy to understand information to help people fight climate change.

Garver, understandably, received some pushback[lviii]. Space Exploration, especially where resource mining and solutions such as space based solar power collectors and helium 3 fueled fusion power plants, provide a better way to combat climate change.

"A better idea than turning NASA into a climate change corps to be sent out to pester people in the hinterlands about how much carbon dioxide they emit exists. The space agency should be tasked to do what it does best: to explore the solar system in partnership with international space agencies and commercial companies."

Still. considering his ceaseless rhetoric about climate change, it would have been understandable if President Biden had chosen the Garver plan rather than stick with NASA's traditional role of space exploration. Indeed, one of the first personnel actions that Biden took was to name a Senior Climate Advisor to the space agency.

However, the first indication that the politics of returning to the moon had changed took the form of a letter sent to the Biden administration by a group of ten Senate Democrats[lix]. The letter urged "robust" funding for the Artemis Program, especially the commercially derived Human Landing System portion.

"Major space exploration efforts have faced disruption as administrations have changed and priorities shifted. It is now time for stability if the nation is to make progress on these initiatives. NASA has made significant progress through the Artemis Program and we strongly believe that those efforts should continue in FY 2022. The program has strong, bipartisan Congressional support and has received nearly $1.5 billion in funding between FY 2020 and FY 2021 in the Commerce, Justice, Science, and Related Agencies Appropriations bills. We recommend robust funding in FY 2022 for continuation of the HLS program and the timely selection of companies to advance to the next stage of development and demonstration contracts. Maintaining competition in this program to the maximum practical extent encourages innovation, controls costs, and ensures the nation has assured access to deep space."

The letter went on to lay out a coherent rationale for returning astronauts to the moon.

"Since its inception, the Artemis Program has captured the excitement and investment of U.S. industry, inspired students, energized STEM programs, and sparked new international partnerships and commitments. Additionally, NASA's SOFIA mission recently discovered even more compelling evidence of water on the Moon, this time in its sunlit regions, affording exciting new opportunities for lunar science.1

"Artemis and HLS will also undeniably support economic recovery, and will provide significant new and expanded opportunities for our national aerospace industrial base and supply chain. In an economic impact study released by the agency in the September 2020, NASA's Moon to Mars initiative, which includes Artemis, created over 69,000 jobs and more than $14 billion of economic output in FY 2019 alone.2 With HLS development beginning in earnest in FY 2021, these figures will undoubtedly rise. Artemis and HLS also support continued U.S. global space leadership. In 2019, China became the third nation after the U.S. and the Soviet Union to successfully complete a soft landing on the lunar surface and they recently conducted a successful sample return mission. China plans to continue to conduct robotic lunar missions over the next few years and build lunar infrastructure with its International Lunar Research Station, and other countries, including India and Israel, have interest in future missions. This presents opportunities for important international collaboration and healthy competition.

"NASA's Artemis Program will return America to deep space, support economic recovery, strengthen national security, promote scientific research, and inspire the next generation. The HLS Program will develop 21st century crewed lunar landers – a critical piece of the Artemis architecture. We urge you to proceed with the planned selection and to include all necessary funding for HLS in your FY 2022 budget request."

The letter was remarkable not only in the depth of its support for the Artemis Program but in the fact that all of the signatories were Democrats. It could be assumed that the vast majority of Republican lawmakers support the effort to return astronauts to the moon. The letter proved that support in Congress for Artemis was both wide and deep.

The same day that the senators sent their letter, according to a story in Ars Technica[lx], Kristin Fisher, a reporter for Fox News and the daughter of two shuttle astronauts, asked about the Biden Administration's support for Artemis at the daily White House press briefing to White House Press Secretary Jen Psaki. Psaki offered her personal support for Artemis and promised to get back with an answer once briefed by Biden's science team.

The following day, Psaki led the briefing with the following statement:

"Through the Artemis Program, the United States will work with industry and international partners to send astronauts to the surface of the Moon—another man and a woman to the Moon, which is very exciting—conduct new and exciting science, prepare for future missions to Mars, and demonstrate America's values. To date, only 12 humans have walked on the Moon— that was half a century ago. The Artemis Program, a waypoint to Mars, provides the opportunity to add numbers to that. Lunar exploration has broad and bicameral support in Congress, most recently detailed in the FY2021 omnibus spending bill, and certainly we support this effort and endeavor."

To be sure, some details were missing from the statement, such as the amount of money the Biden administration would propose for Artemis. Also, Psaki did not reveal who the administration might be thinking of nominating for NASA chief. Still, along with the support from Senate Democrats, the White House statement was more than encouraging for supporters of the Artemis program and a return to the moon.

Why has Artemis prospered when the back to the moon efforts pushed by President George H. W. Bush and President George W. Bush did not survive the end of those two gentlemen's administrations? Very likely, the survival of Artemis had to do with the relentless selling of the program to both sides of the political divide by Jim Bridenstine when he was NASA administrator. Bridenstine, shrewdly, deduced that any transformative space project such as Artemis could not last long if it was supported just by one political party or another. So, he lobbied for the back to the moon program, employing the political skills and contacts he had developed as a member of Congress.

When Bridenstine was undergoing his tendentious confirmation process, the main slam against him was that he was a politician. He was not, in the words of Sen. Bill Nelson, his chief inquisitor, an "aerospace professional."

The irony, therefore, could not be more apparent in that the quality that Senate Democrats saw as most problematic in Bridenstine proved to be the very thing that helped him preserve the Artemis program, even past his term as NASA administrator. No former astronaut, aerospace company executive, or NASA middle manager would likely to have been so successful. Only a politician who understood the language of politics could have saved Artemis from the fate that its predecessors suffered.

Another sign that Artemis is real stems from the fact that the mainstream media has finally decided to notice that the United States has a back to the moon program 60 Minutes, CBS's long running TV news magazine, ran a segment[lxi] on the idea that Artemis is not only named after the twin sister of Apollo but has a number of women in highly placed positions in the program.

The segment featured Charlie Blackwell-Thompson, NASA's first female flight director, and Jody Singer, the first female director of the Marshall Space Flight Center. Oddly, the segment did not feature Kathy Lueders, the associate administrator for human space exploration and operations, but did include Lori Garver. Garver seemed to have dropped her idea of making NASA a climate change organization. She did criticize the Space Launch System as too expensive, suggesting that NASA return to the moon using commercial launch vehicles like the SpaceX Falcon Heavy and eventually the Starship.

In short, while the Biden Administration was relentlessly overturning a great many Trump policies, it had embraced the Artemis program. The development was unique in the history of previous lunar efforts, including Apollo, which started under a Democrat named Kennedy, was executed by another Democrat named Johnson, and was wound down by a Republican named Nixon. Biden, a Democrats, had made Artemis, a policy enacted by a Republican named Donald Trump, his own.

Chapter 13: The hunt for a new NASA Administrator and a new space policy

2021

One of the first orders of business the Biden Administration had for putting its stamp on space policy was to choose a new NASA Administrator. Early indications suggested that President Biden wanted to choose a woman, according to rumors reported by Space.com[lxii].

Hiring a woman would fit very much with the Biden Administration's policy of doing diversity hires. Biden's vice president, Kamala Harris, had been picked because of her identity as a "woman of color." The fact that she had taken down Biden as a racist during a debate was forgotten.

A number of well qualified women existed who would make fine NASA administrators, Kathy Lueders, Associate Administrator for Human Exploration and Operations, comes to mind[lxiii].

A number of women, however, would be problematic. Kendra Horn, a one term member of Congress who had authored a NASA authorization bill that would have crippled the Artemis program, was one example. Lori Garver, who had served as Deputy Administrator of NASA under President Obama and had been blamed for the destruction of the Bush 43 era Constellation program, was another.

Toward the end of February 2021, another, somewhat unusual name arose in a social media rumor.[lxiv]

"RUMINT: Former Sen. Bill Nelson (Fla.) is said to be Biden admin pick for NASA administrator, killing several birds with one stone: strong relationship with POTUS, congressional savvy. Pam Melroy is on deck as his deputy, bringing technical chops to bear."

Pam Melroy is a former NASA astronaut and has also served in the military and at DARPA. However, as Ars Technica reported, Bill Nelson as NASA Administrator would be --- interesting.[lxv]

Nelson, it should be remembered, excoriated the very idea that Jim Bridenstine should be the NASA Administrator because Bridenstine was a politician and not an "aerospace professional." Nelson had also used his political muscle to force his way onto a space shuttle mission in the 1980s. Now, Nelson was using his connection with President Biden as former senators together to get the job at NASA,

One revelation that did come to light that made Nelson as NASA Administrator problematic was that he had invested in a Chinese telecom company that had been blacklisted by the Defense Department[lxvi]. He had also been a warm supporter of space cooperation with the Beijing regime. Both facts, in view of the Chinese human rights violations, its imperial drive for world domination, and its lack of transparency concerning the origins of the coronavirus, counted against Nelson's appointment to run the space agency.

By the middle of the last week of February 2021, the White House shot down the Nelson trial balloon. It announced that it had no near-term plans to nominate a new NASA Administrator.[lxvii]

However, by the middle of March, the Biden administration announced that it would indeed nominate Bill Nelson to be NASA Administrator[lxviii]. The reaction was decidedly mixed, to put the matter mildly.

On the one hand, Nelson's nomination garnered a great deal of support, not only from politicians such as Sen. Marco Rubio, who tweeted[lxix], "Bill Nelson would be an excellent pick to lead @NASA" but a number of organizations such as the National Space Society[lxx] and the Commercial Spaceflight Federation.

On the other hand, Marina Koren, writing for The Atlantic, took a dim view of the nomination, primarily because the Biden Administration had chosen to renege on its promise to name a woman to the post of NASA Administrator.[lxxi]

Lori Garver, the Obama-era Deputy Administrator of NASA, was even less pleased, according to Florida Today[lxxii]. She noted Nelson's role in creating the super heavy Space Launch System.

"His legacy is the monster rocket & in some ways it is poetic justice that it will be his cross to bear." She went on to wonder, "If he'd had his way, commercial crew wouldn't have existed - just SLS/Orion. The guy who undermined the Dems & bet on the wrong horse gets rewarded?"

Garver left out her role in the creation of the SLS in the agreement she called a "Faustian bargain."[lxxiii]

Nelson received what was on the surface an unusual endorsement.[lxxiv]

"Former NASA Administrator Jim Bridenstine today released the following statement after the Biden administration nominated Senator Bill Nelson to lead NASA.

"'Bill Nelson is an excellent pick for NASA Administrator. He has the political clout to work with President Biden's Office of Management and Budget, National Security Council, Office of Science and Technology Policy, and bipartisan Members of the House and Senate. He has the diplomatic skills to lead an international coalition sustainably to the Moon and on to Mars. Bill Nelson will have the influence to deliver strong budgets for NASA and, when necessary, he will be able to enlist the help of his friend, President Joe Biden. The Senate should confirm Bill Nelson without delay.'''

Bridenstine obviously set aside personal considerations for what he saw as the greater good. He had used his political skills to steer NASA and the Artemis program to good effect. But would Nelson, who could be described as a swamp creature, leave behind some of his tendency to make poor choices and do the same? The jury, upon his nomination, was still out.

Even though the Artemis program had gotten bipartisan support in the United States, that did not mean that no opposition existed. Elon Musk tweeted[lxxv], "I am accumulating resources to help make life multiplanetary & extend the light of consciousness to the stars"

The tweet triggered Sen. Bernie Sanders, I-Vermont, who responded quite caustically.[lxxvi]

"Space travel is an exciting idea, but right now we need to focus on Earth and create a progressive tax system so that children don't go hungry, people are not homeless and all

Americans have healthcare. The level of inequality in America is obscene and a threat to our democracy.”

Sanders was echoing opposition to space exploration that has occurred on the left since the Apollo program. The twist was that the “democratic socialist” senator was not just opposing government funded space exploration, but such conducted even by a private person with his own money. The implicit threat was that Sanders would tax away Musk’s money so that he would be unable to pursue his dreams of building a city on Mars. Instead, his wealth would be used for purposes that Sanders approved of.

Robert Reich, former Secretary of Labor under President Bill Clinton and current professor at Berkeley, offered much the same assessment:[lxxvii]

“We don't need Musk to ‘extend the light of consciousness to the stars’. We need him to pay his fair share in taxes so people living on *this planet* can survive and thrive.”

While space exploration, including the Artemis program, seemed to have achieved bipartisan support in the early days of the Biden Administration, Sanders and Reich proved that the support was not universal. Also, unlike the opposition to Apollo which focused on government spending, the leftwing pushback concerned a private citizen who was using his own money to achieve a dream of settling Mars. The reaction by Sanders and Reich proved, if nothing else, that there is nothing democratic in “democratic socialism.” The sentiments expressed by the senator and the academic were very authoritarian.

As March 2021 drew to a close, the Biden administration decided to retain the National Space Council. The Council was a body of cabinet level officials that was revived by President Trump in order to coordinate space policy across the federal government. Its retention was a sign that the Biden White House was serious about space as a venue of policy.

The Biden Administration’s embrace of Artemis did not mean that everyone was happy about its approach. Washington Post reporter Christian Davenport revealed[lxxviii] that Rep. Eddie Bernice Johnson, D-Texas, the chair of the House Science and Technology Committee, had sent a letter to President Biden demanding that the selection of commercially developed and operated Human Landing Systems, aka lunar landers, be deferred. She, in effect, demanded that the Biden Administration take an action that was required in HR 5666, the NASA Authorization bill, that had failed so spectacularly in the previous congress.

The first details of a Biden administration approach to Artemis came when it released its first budget proposal for FY 2022.[lxxix] The language read as follows:

“**Supports Human Exploration of the Moon, Mars, and Beyond**. The discretionary request provides $6.9 billion, an increase of $325 million above the 2021 enacted level, for the Artemis program, a series of crewed exploration missions to the lunar surface and beyond. This funding supports the development of capabilities for sustainable, long duration human exploration beyond Earth, and eventually to Mars.”

The proposed spending increased appeared to be modest, suggesting a go-slow approach. The language made no mention of a permanent lunar base, a matter of some concern.

The selection of the SpaceX "lunar starship" as the Human Landing System that would, at least, deliver the first American astronauts to the moon's surface in over 50 years raised more than a few eyebrows. NASA had been expected to choose two proposals just as it had for Commercial Crew. However, the stinginess of Congress in appropriating money for the HLS forced the space agency to choose just one[lxxx]. Nevertheless, the two losing teams, Dynetics and Blue Origin, filed complaints with the General Accounting Office.

Not only was SpaceX the low bidder, but also NASA was impressed by the quality of the lunar starship's design" and the quality of the country's management. The SpaceX proposal would constitute quite a challenge as it would require multiple refueling events to get the vehicle to the lunar surface with cargo and crew. Also, the first moonwalkers would have to ride an elevator to the surface rather than climb down a ladder as had been the case during Apollo.

Also, the SpaceX HLS encountered potentially political difficulties. The chair of the House Science and Technology Committee, Rep. Eddie Bernice Johnson, D-Texas, expressed her displeasure.[lxxxi]

"I am disappointed that the Acting NASA leadership decided to make such a consequential award prior to the arrival of a new permanent NASA Administrator and Deputy Administrator. The decision to make the award today also comes despite the obvious need for a re-baselining of NASA's lunar exploration program, which has no realistic chance of returning U.S. astronauts to the Moon by 2024. While work continues on the upcoming Artemis-1 mission, it will be critically important for the new NASA leadership team to carry out its own review of all elements of NASA's Moon-Mars initiative to ensure that this major national undertaking is put on a sound footing."

The matter of the SpaceX lunar lander came up during Bill Nelson's confirmation hearings. Senate Commerce Committee Chair Maria Cantwell, D-Washington was decidedly unhappy. She suggested that NASA should find a way to pick two contractors, even though Congress had appropriated only enough money for one.

Still. the hearings, in contrast to those that attended Jim Bridenstine's nomination, were a love fest for Nelson, greeted by many of his former Senate colleagues as a conquering hero. Nelson, for his part, advocated continuality for NASA space policy rather than a change of direction. He approved of the commercial crew program, the Artemis program, the Artemis Accords, Earth Science spending, and ethnic and gender diversity at the space agency. He even took time to praise Jim Bridenstine, a man he once excoriated, and pledged to seek his advice from time to time.

It looked like that Nelson, who often used his political skills for dubious purposes, might just, in the twilight of his life, use them for good. When he was sworn in on May 3, 2021, by Vice President Kamala Harris, who had assumed chairmanship of the National Space Council, Nelson stressed continuity and bipartisanship. Charles Bolden and Jim Bridenstine were in attendance, albeit the latter in virtual form.

Just like the space station, returning to the moon had been fraught with controversy and political acrimony. Just like the ISS, Artemis had become something warmly supported by everyone regardless of party affiliation. Bridenstin did that, though Nelson gets lots of credit for recognizing and supporting the new reality. The prospect of Americans returning to the moon never seemed brighter.

Chapter 14: Why should America return to the moon?

The question of whether America is going back to the moon has apparently been settled. The reason why America should return to the moon has been asked and answered in a number of ways ever since the Apollo program concluded with a victory over the Soviet Union. The answer, however, needs articulating so that all doubt can be swept away, and the project can proceed.

In general, the reasons America is returning to the moon is, like Gaul, is divided into three parts. Those reasons are science[lxxxii], commerce[lxxxiii], and soft political power[lxxxiv].

Science is rather obvious. The moon is a great venue for astronauts to study geology and geophysics, science that requires human beings on the scene. The scientific study of the moon had already helped to answer questions about the formation of the moon and the history of the early solar system.

The moon could also serve as a platform for science. One proposal would be to build a radio telescope on the far side of the moon[lxxxv]. Such a facility would be able to observe the universe in wavelengths that are ordinarily reflected by the Earth's atmosphere. It would also be shieled from radio noise from Earth by the moon's mass. The capabilities of such a lunar radio telescope would far outstrip anything built on the Earth's surface.

The moon is the repository of a great deal of natural resources. Water ice, which can be refined into rocket fuel and use to support lunar settlers, resides at the moon's pole. Helium 3 could be used to fuel clean, limitless fusion energy[lxxxvi]. The moon also holds industrial metals such as iron, titanium, and aluminum, platinum group metals, and rare earths that could help spark a space-based industrial revolution.

But the one, overriding reason to return to the moon will be to retain the position of the United States as the supreme superpower on Earth. Artemis will accomplish this goal in a slightly different way than Apollo did during the 1960s race to the moon.

Apollo was a primarily American project meant to overawe the rest of the world with the ability of the United States to send a man to the moon and bring him safely back to the Earth. Apollo succeeded beyond the wildest dreams of President John F. Kennedy, demonstrating the technological and economic superiority of the United States over the Soviet Union.

Artemis will approach the problem differently. The modern race to the moon features the United States seeking allies and partners, not only other countries but commercial firms such as SpaceX. The message is that if a country joins the United States in returning to the moon, it will participate in the greatest adventure of the 21st Century, so far. It means the European, Asian, and even Middle Eastern astronauts can hope to live and work on the moon, alongside their American counterparts. Be America's friend and you too can help to open the high frontier of space.

Just as during the sixties, the United States is involved in a space race, albeit a different one that occurred over fifty years ago. The Russian Federation and the People's Republic of China are forming what amounts to a Sino-Russian Space Axis to oppose the American led Artemis Alliance[lxxxvii]. The prize is not bragging rights over who is first back to the moon. The prize of the 21st Century space race will be which side best uses the moon for the betterment of humankind.

The latest effort to return not only Americans but American allies to the moon comes at a tumultuous time in history. As of this writing, a pandemic has swept the world, causing economic and social dislocation and no few deaths. The United States has been roiled by racial animus, brought on by police shootings, and a crisis on the southern border. A new president is proposing tax and spending programs that many believe will cripple the American economy. Climate change and what to do about it remain burning issues.

For the first time in many decades, the support for a return to the moon has become bipartisan. President Donald Trump began Project Artemis. President Joe Biden has pledged to continue it.

Still, support for Artemis is not universal. Senate Bernie Sanders, I-Vermont, considered the leader of the "Democratic Socialist" wing of the Democratic Party, raised an old specter that had dogged the Apollo program. During the 2020 presidential campaign, his campaign website stated, "Bernie supports NASA's mission and is generally in favor of increasing funding for NASA, but only after the needs of Americans on Earth are met first."[lxxxviii]

The statement contained echoes of politicians on the left, such as Walter Mondale, who condemned spending on space exploration and demanded that money be spent on social programs instead. Mondale recently died at the age of 93.

Sanders even spoke out against private individuals using their own money to open up the high frontier of space. The implication was clear. Musk and people like him should have their wealth taxed away so that Sanders and his like could spend the money on social programs.

As I described in my book, *Why is it so Hard to Go Back to the Moon,* [lxxxix]politicians on the left successfully inveighed to have the Apollo program truncated and much of what was planned to happen afterwards stillborn. As a result, not one of the societal ills such politicians cited has been solved. Indeed, many have been made worse. And humans have not been back to the moon since 1972, not to mention to Mars.

Will the Artemis Alliance of free nations and commercial companies spread our species and civilization beyond the Earth this time? The future of the Earth and its inhabitants resides in the balance.

\Notes

i President John F. Kennedy Address to a Joint Session of Congress, May 25, 1961, JFK Library

ii President John F. Kennedy Rice University Moon Speech, September 12, 1962

iii Analyzing the New Kennedy Tape, John Logsdon, The Space Review, May 31, 2011

iv President John F. Kennedy Address before the UN General Assembly, September 20, 1963

v Pioneering the Space Frontier: The Report on the National Commission on Space, NASA

vi NASA Leadership and America's Future in Space, Dr. Sally Ride

vii Remarks on the 20th Anniversary of the Apollo 11 Moon landing, President George H. W. Bush, July 20, 1989

viii Mars Wars: The Rise and Fall of the Space Exploration Initiative, Thor Hogan

ix Why is it so Hard to go back to the Moon?, Mark R. Whittington, 2015

x Remarks at the Texas A&I University Commencement Ceremony in Kingsville, President George H. W. Bush, May 11, 1990

xi President Bush delivers Remarks on U.S. Space Policy, President George W. Bush, January 14, 2004, NASA

xii Getting to Know Michael Griffin, Jeff Foust, The Space Review, March 14, 2005

xiii A Cold War Mystery: Why Did Jimmy Carter Save the Space Shuttle, Eric Berger, Ars Technica, July 14, 2016

xiv Seeking a Human Spaceflight Program Worthy of a Great Nation, Norm Augustine, et al

xv Remarks by the President on Space Exploration in the 21st Century, President Barack Obama, April 15, 2010

xvi To Save on Weight a Detour to the Moon is the Best Route to Mars, Jennifer Chu, MIT News, October 14, 2015

xvii Restore the Teaching of American Exceptionalism In the Classroom, The Heritage Foundation, August 28, 2020

xviii Asteroid Expert Richard Binzel: ARM is Emperor with No Clothes, Len Ly, Spacepolicyonline.com. August 1, 2014

xix Newt Gingrich Reaffirms Support for Moon Mining in Presidential Debate, Mike Wall, Space.com, December 10, 2011

xx Transcript of Newt Gingrich January 25 Space Policy Speech, David Brandt-Erichsen, NSS, January 25, 2012

xxi Romney tells Gingrich: I'd fire you for your moon proposal, Stephanie Condon, CBS News, January 27, 2012

xxii Mike Griffin, Romney Space Advisors, Keith Cowing, NASA Watch, January 12, 2012

xxiii How Newt Gingrich's moon base became 'pretty cool', Mark R. Whittington, the Hill, October 21, 2015

xxiv Space Policy Directive 1, Federal Register, December 11, 2017

xxv Trump: "I want to rebuild our infrastructure before sending people to Mars", Marcia Smith, Space Policy Online, August 15, 2015

xxvi Trump: "Look at your space program…we're like a third world nation", Eric Berger, Ars Technica, August 3, 2016

xxvii Will Trump pick an "agent of change" or an insider to lead NASA?, Eric Berger, Ars Technica, November 17, 2016

xxviii NASA Statement on National Space Council Policy for Future American Leadership in Space, NASA, October 5, 2017

xxix James Bridenstine NASA Administrator Nomination Hearing, Youtube, November 1, 2017

xxx Bridenstine faces partisan criticism at NASA administrator nomination hearing, Jeff Foust, Space News, November 1, 2017

xxxi Bridenstine introduces American Space Renaissance Act, Jeff Foust and Mike Gruss, Space News, April 13, 2016

xxxii H.R. 4945 American Space Renaissance Act, Congress.gov

xxxiii Bridenstine: This Is Our Sputnik Moment & The Moon Will Ensure American Preeminence in Space, Marcia Smith, Space Policy Online, November 3, 2016

xxxiv Jim Bridenstine for NASA Administrator, Mark R. Whittington. The Hill, February 2, 2017

xxxv Bernie Sanders Tweet, September 15, 2020

xxxvi Commercial Orbital Transportation Services, NASA

xxxvii How Much Value Can SpaceX Unlock From Starlink's Proposed IPO, Forbes, February 14, 2020

xxxviii US to Return Astronauts to the Moon by 2024, VP Pence Says, Mike Wall, Space.com. 2019

xxxix Lawmakers Grill NASA Chief on Moon-By-2024 Budget, Schedule, Meghan Bartels, Space.com, October 2019

xl NASA Administrator Selects Douglas Loverro as Next Human Spaceflighty Head, NASA, October 16, 2019

xli Here's why NASA's chief of human spaceflight resigned --- and why it matters, Eric Berger, Ars Technica, May 20, 2020

[xlii] NASA Authorization Bill of 2020, House Science Committee

[xliii] Letter from Concerned Scientists Regarding H.R. 5666, Space Ref, January 31, 2020

[xliv] CSF Statement on House Space Subcommittee NASA Authorization Bill, Tommy Sanford, Commercial Space Federation, January 26, 2020

[xlv] NASA Authorization Bill Update, Jim Bridenstine, NASA, January 27, 2020

[xlvi] House legislators want to hand NASA's spaceflight program over to Boeing, Eric Berger, Ars Technica, January 27, 2020

[xlvii] Trump's 2024 moon goal faces 'challenge' in Senate, GOP chair predicts, Jacqueline Feldscher, Politico, July 31, 2020

[xlviii] The Artemis Accords, NASA

[xlix] Eight countries sign Artemis Accords, Jeff Foust, Space News, October 12, 2020

[l] Artemis Accords: why many countries are refusing to sign moon exploration agreement, Christopher Newsman, Space.com, October 2020

[li] For sale: The Moon, Stephen Bouno, the Hill, October 20, 2020

[lii] The Artemis Accords take shape, Jeff Foust, The Space Review, October 26, 2020

[liii] 2020 Democratic Party platform endorses Trump's NASA moon program, Mark Whittington, The Hill, August 2, 2020

[liv] President-elect Biden names 8-person NASA transition team, Mike Wall, Space.com. November 2020

[lv] Biden administration expected to emphasize climate science over lunar exploration at NASA, Jeff Foust, Space News, November 9, 2020

[lvi] Imagine what NASA could do to solve the climate crisis, Lori Garver, Seattle Times, July 19, 2019

[lvii] Earthrise Alliance

[lviii] Let NASA keep exploring space, Mark Whittington, Washington Examiner, August 5, 2019

[lix] Letter from U.S. Senators to President Biden Regarding NASA's Human Landing System (HLS) Program, Space.Ref, February 3, 2021

[lx] White House says its supports Artemis Program to return to the Moon, Eric Berger, Ars Technica, February 4, 2021

[lxi] NASA's New Race to Put a Woman on the Moon, Bill Whitaker, CBS News, March 7, 2021

[lxii] Is NASA about to get its first female leader?, Mike Wall, Space.com. January 2021

[lxiii] Biden should choose Kathy Lueders as his NASA Administrator, Mark Whittington, Washington Examiner, November 12, 2020

[lxiv] Breaking Defense, Twitter, February 22, 2021

[lxv] A politician who said politicians shouldn't run NASA wants to run NASA, Eric Berge, Ars Technica, February 23, 2021

[lxvi] Potential Biden NASA Pick Invested in Chinese Telecom Giant Blacklisted by Pentagon, Jack Beyrer, Washington Free Beacon, February 25, 2021

[lxvii] White House not making near-term plans to nominate a NASA Administrator, Jeff Foust, Space News, February 23, 2021

[lxviii] President Biden Announcing his Intent to Nominate Bill Nelson for the National Aeronautics and Space Administration, White House, March 19, 2021

[lxix] Marco Rubio, Twitter, March 18, 2021

[lxx] Michelle L. D. Hanlon, Twitter March 22, 2021

[lxxi] There's Nothing Historic about Biden's NASA Pick, Marina Koren, The Atlantic, March 19, 2021

[lxxii] Nelson's nomination to head NASA draws both cheers and jeers, Rachael Joy, Florida Today, March 21, 2021

[lxxiii] Unleashing the Dragon – the NASA bargain behind this week's SpaceX Launch, Lori Garver and Michael Sheetz, CNBC, May 26, 2021

[lxxiv] Former NASA Administrator Jim Bridenstine's Comments on Bill Nelson's nomination, Jim Bridenstine, Spaceref, March 19, 2021

[lxxv] Elon Musk, Twitter, March 21, 2021

[lxxvi] Sen. Bernie Sanders, Twitter, March 21, 2021

[lxxvii] Robert Reich, Twitter March 22, 2021

lxxviii Christian Davenport, Twitter, April 5, 2021

lxxix President's Request for FY 2022 Budget, Office of Management and Budget, April 9, 2021

lxxx As Artemis Moves Forward, NASA Picks SpaceX to Land the Next Americans on the Moon, NASA April 16, 2021

lxxxi Chairwoman Johnson Statement On NASA's Artemis Human Landing System Award, Rep. Bernice Johnson, D-Texas, House Science Committee, April 16, 2021

lxxxii Going back to the moon for science, Mark Whittington, the Hill, April 12, 2019

lxxxiii Returning to the moon for rocket fuel and clean energy, Mark Whittington, the Hill, April 19, 2019

lxxxiv Returning to the moon for soft political power, Mark Whittington, the Hill, April 27, 2019

lxxxv Replace the Arecibo radio telescope with one on the moon's far side, Mark Whittington, December 20, 2020

lxxxvi Solving the climate and energy crises: Mine the Moon's helium-3?, Mark Whittington, February 28, 2021

lxxxvii The new race to the moon: the Artemis Alliance vs the Sino-Russian Axis, Mark Whittington, March 28, 2021

lxxxviii Sanders NASA plan is definitely Earth first, Mark Whittington, the Hill, September 10, 2019